The
Rite
Thing

A TOWER
BOOK

The Rite Thing

EUGENE BRAND

AUGSBURG PUBLISHING HOUSE
MINNEAPOLIS, MINNESOTA

THE RITE THING

Manufactured in the United States of America

To my parents
who took me to worship

Foreword

A tower has both height and strength. Grounded in a firm foundation, it provides the opportunity for a full-range perspective and soaring vision. It was in a tower that Luther had the shattering experience of grace which began the Reformation with its insights into the Gospel of God and new freedoms for man.

Volumes in the Tower Book series aspire to this image. They seek to serve the curious and reflective Christian by examining the varied themes of God and man in clear, concise, and interesting (perhaps even sparkling) ways. Committed to the biblical faith, the various authors explore great ideas, reflect on the application of the faith to daily life, transmit the wisdom of inspiring thinkers in the past, suggest new strategy for the church in the world, and open up the Scriptures as honestly and competently as they can.

Each author is different and writes from his own "tower" and in his own style. You, the reader, read against the background of your own experience, of course.

Being a Christian in the modern age is an exciting enterprise. It requires both diligence and knowledge. For this task we all need the help and counsel of others.

Take and read.

And joy to you!

Kent S. Knutson
Editor, Tower Books

Preface

Worship is becoming increasingly difficult for many people today. Questions are raised about its relevance to modern life. Some regard it as a comforting escape from the harshness of real life. Others see in it proof that the church always lags far behind the culture of the "now generation."

But the fact remains that worship is essential to Christian existence, and that Christians simply must cope with the problems raised above. This book attempts to shed light upon the action of worship itself, and also upon the relationship it has to the Christian life as a whole. It goes without saying that reform of the shape of the liturgy must proceed from a clear understanding of what corporate worship itself is. The theological question is not necessarily prior to the liturgical one, but they are intimately related. Where the theological question is ignored, reform often means mere whimsical puttering.

My gratitude goes to the staff and participants of the *Schola Cantorum* Festival Week, Concordia Semi-

nary, St. Louis, to whom much of the substance of
these chapters was first delivered. Their reactions and
questions have been most helpful.

Thanks are also due the following publishers for
permission to quote from the works indicated: Harcourt, Brace and World, Inc. for *Murder in the Cathedral*, G. P. Putnam's Sons for *The Upper Hand*, Herder
and Herder for *Footnotes and Headlines*, Fortress
Press for *Luther's Works* (Vol. 53), Alphonse Leduc for
Litanies, and the Oxford University Press for *Worship,
Its Theology and Practice*.

New forms of worship tend toward more flexibility
and a greater degree of participation by the people—
both real strides forward. But this developing situation
makes increased creative demands of clergy, musicians, artists, and people. Toward the goal of facilitating their participation this contribution is offered.

Columbus, Ohio   Eugene Brand
October 1969

Contents

*The last temptation is the greatest treason:
To do the right deed for the wrong reason.*

T. S. Eliot, *Murder in the Cathedral**

. . the rite thing for the rote reason. . . .

J. W. Corrington, *The Upper Hand***

*By permission of Harcourt, Brace & World, Inc.
**Copyright © 1967 G. P. Putnam's.

Prologue

Shortly before noon each Sunday morning Christians all over the world gather to do their thing. Traditionalists call it worship. What they do has its origin more than nineteen centuries ago in the rites of the earliest Christians. Why do they do it? Surely there must be a reason, especially since it has had such tenacity. Or is it just a habit, an almost meaningless gesture?

T. S. Eliot puts memorable words in the mouth of Thomas à Becket as he contemplates martyrdom: "The last temptation is the greatest treason: To do the right deed for the wrong reason." If worship is good in itself is that justification enough for participating? Or must one know why, must there be a right reason?

On a summer's morning in New Orleans, in the midst of his morning mass, Father Christopher Nieman turns from the altar and walks out of the church and the priesthood. Novelist J. W. Corrington draws him as a disillusioned clergyman. Father Nieman is convinced that his people are just going through motions which have no significance in their real lives. They are people—himself included—doing the rite thing for the rote reason.

Christian worship can be inspiring and exciting. The rite can be a vital experience. To deny that would be to deny testimony from countless spiritual biographies. But the rite can also be a dull, mechanical action performed by a flock of docile sheep and led by a properly programmed shepherd. Such rote worship is what critics of the church decry and what too many churchgoers experience.

Christian worship should be a celebration in joyous commemoration of the most significant event in our history: the death and resurrection of Jesus. People should participate because they can't help responding to the significance of the event in their lives. They should find the rite a natural and necessary expression of a joy which must be shared. That is the ideal.

The ideal situation does occur—but not always, not for everyone. But if faith is vital, and if people participate intelligently, the ideal is more likely to be reached. The chapters which follow deal with themes basic to Christian worship. Reading them will not automatically result in more intelligent worship, but using them as a stimulus to more thought and reading will help.

1.

To be involved . . .

Zoom in on one fan among the thousands at a major league game. There he sits, beer in hand, absorbed in the action on the diamond below. But he isn't passive. He lives the game. He participates, at least vocally, in what happens. He's a bit flushed both from the beer and the yelling, in his mid-thirties, with a waistline beginning to expand, loyal to the game, loves the action, wouldn't be anywhere else on a summer Sunday afternoon.

Portrait of a spectator—ardent exponent of athletics who never gets closer than the grandstands, the sports page, or the TV screen.

Reload the camera and zoom in on another fellow, also over thirty, but of a rarer breed. Photography will be more difficult because this man is in motion on the tennis court. He's a bit trimmer than our grandstand sportsman, and not a bad player. He enjoys watching a game as much as the next man, but he would really rather be in there himself. He thinks of athletics primarily as playing the game, being involved.

Portrait of a participant. It could be any sport—golf, basketball, handball, swimming, even jogging—but somehow when he talks about it the words ring truer, have a more authentic tone.

Both men benefit from their exposure to sports. The spectator enjoys watching, finds it entertaining, experiences the game as a kind of catharsis. He may react to the situations on the field with emotion as intense as any player's. But it is a momentary diversion, a break in the routine. It has little ongoing effect upon his life apart from fulfilling his need for diversion.

The participant gets all this and more. A good game of tennis is also a pleasant diversion from the routine, but because the player is actually involved in the game it benefits him physically and mentally as well. He emerges from his shower relaxed and refreshed, a bit more fit than before and better able to take on the world again.

It may seem strange to begin a discussion of worship with a homily on athletics. But perhaps it is already obvious that the homily could apply to worship as well. Any group of Christians assembled for worship has both spectators and participants. Unfortunately, in most instances, spectators predominate.

In fact, the first part of the sketch can be carried even farther. Where there are spectators a game is being played. There are participants. They are the highly skilled professionals playing games for others to watch. In many congregations a similar situation prevails. Spectators gather to watch the professionals, clergy and musicians, play the liturgical game. As good spectators they may be well informed about the rules and the qualifications of the players. They may become quite absorbed in the action and participate in it vocally. And when it is over they may have derived the usual spectator benefits: entertainment and emotional release.

It cannot be said, therefore, that spectator-worshipers get nothing from the service. Nor can it be said that being spectators makes them hypocrites. Perhaps they have been led to believe that no adult who is not a pro (not ordained) participates in the action of the liturgy. Perhaps they think that being a spectator is the proper role for the laity. Our culture reinforces the spectator orientation. Many an ardent baseball fan over thirty would feel self-conscious and a bit foolish actually playing the game in the presence of an audience. After all, only kids and pros play ball. And many a layman would feel just as reticent about reading the Epistle or distributing the elements in Holy Communion. Only pastors do that.

The interior arrangement of our churches underlines the spectator orientation. The pews are arranged little differently from seats in a sports arena or theater. They suggest an audience gathered to watch others do something. So long as worship takes place in such surroundings it will remain difficult to change the basic orientation of the congregation.

Is the participant orientation possible? Can the congregation actually engage in the action more than mentally and vocally? Can the pews become player benches rather than audience seats?

Action!

Using the analogy with athletics assumes that worship is action. That assumption may be challenged and therefore need some defense.

In sketching the spectator orientation the attempt was made to avoid simple condemnation. But the sketch was obviously slanted in favor of the participant. If the congregation is to join in, worship must be action, the kind of action in which groups of amateurs can engage. It must be a team sport which does not require rare or exceptional skills. Otherwise it would be folly to speak about participation (as that term is commonly understood)

When Christian worship first emerged all participants were either Jews or closely connected with Judaism. According to the Acts of the Apostles, the earliest Christians still participated in the services of the temple. In addition, they gathered in someone's house for the breaking of bread (Acts 2:46). Outside Jerusalem, the synagogue and the assembly for the Lord's Supper were the normal points of focus.

Because of the missionary activities of St. Paul and

others, and as a result of strife between the followers of Jesus and Judaism, a break occurred between the Followers of the Way and the institutions of Jewish worship. But the synagogue had left its imprint upon Christian worship. When its doors were closed to Christians their worship was not simply reduced to gathering for the Lord's Supper alone. They amplified this specifically Christian action to include elements of the synagogue service.

In time a structure developed which contained two points of focus: one upon the verbal forms of reading from the Scriptures and preaching, the other upon the Lord's Supper itself. These were surrounded, following Jewish tradition, with songs of praise and with prayers of intercession and thanksgiving. In its mature form there have been many names for this structure: the Holy Eucharist, the Sacred Liturgy, the Mass, the Holy Communion, the Divine Service. But throughout the world and over the centuries it has been divisible into two halves: the office of the word (patterned after the synagogue) and the office of the eucharist (patterned after the upper room).

During the formative centuries, then, congregations gathered to do something: to celebrate the resurrection of Jesus by eating the paschal supper together and, as part of this celebration, to read the Scriptures, hear these readings explained and applied, and to pray. All the crucial terms are action words: celebrate, eat, read, hear, pray. In some of them the action is more obvious than in others. But judging from the practice in Corinth, the congregation was really involved, and the action was appropriately rather informal.

> What then, brethren? When you come together, each one has a hymn, a lesson, a revelation, a tongue, or an interpretation. Let all things be done for edification. If any speak in a tongue, let there be only two or at most three, and each in turn; and let one interpret. But if there is no one to interpret, let each of them keep silence in church and speak to himself and to God. Let two or three prophets speak, and let the others weigh what is said. If a revelation is made to another sitting by, let the first be silent. For you can all prophesy one by one, so that all may learn and all be encouraged; and the spirits of prophets are subject to prophets.
>
> 1 Corinthians 14:26-32

Even the term used to describe this worship denotes action: liturgy. In non-biblical Greek usage a liturgical act was one performed as a public service for the benefit of the body politic. A well-to-do citizen might organize and pay for a public ceremony which would include a banquet for the officiants, or he might defray the cost of the chorus at a public feast. Because it was difficult to distinguish between civil and religious rites, such a public act always carried with it cultic overtones. Eventually this term *liturgy* became the technical term used by Greek-speaking Christianity for acts of corporate worship. Beginnings of this are observable in the Greek version of the Old Testament

(Septuagint), and the tenacity of the term can be traced through the history of the Eastern Orthodox Churches where the service is usually called the Divine Liturgy.

The role of the clergyman in the assembly for worship also testified to the involvement of the congregation. His title was president. He presided over an assembly of acting people. Certain acts, such as the eucharistic prayer and the blessings, were reserved to him, but he also regulated and coordinated the individual and corporate acts of the congregation. Spectators do not need a president; a working group of people does.

Active to Passive

By the Middle Ages the clergyman's title had changed from president to celebrant. What seems like a rather insignificant change of titles signals a drastic change in the concept of worship. The celebrant was the pro. He performed the liturgical action for a congregation of spectators. The shift which began during the Constantinian era reached its climax in the Middle Ages. The liturgy had changed from a corporate action to a spectacle. The congregation had changed from participants to spectators.

The shift was not the result of some sort of diabolical plot to destroy worship. It occurred as the church attempted to meet various problems and accommodate itself to various cultural pressures. Another factor was the transition from a strongly eschatological orientation (expecting Jesus' second coming to occur soon) to a historical orientation which sought to Christianize civil and social life.

To defend the purity of the faith it was felt necessary to put the singing of the service in the hands of minor clerics who were more discerning and could be controlled. Heretical movements often employed songs as propaganda devices. Records tell of rival bands of religionists battling for the allegiance of the populace through singing. In several towns Aryans and orthodox Christians "fought" each other by organizing processions which went through the streets singing.

In such a situation it was only natural for heretical hymns to find their way into corporate worship. To guard against this the singing was taken over more and more by minor clerics (the birth of the choir!). The congregation thus lost one important way of participating. Instead of being singers they became listeners.

The Constantinian era brought the liturgical life of the church more into the public eye. Masses of people flocked into the congregations; large and often elegant buildings were erected; Christianity was the prestige religion in the empire and absorbed many Roman customs. All this conspired to make the liturgical action more ritualistic and pompous. It is a tribute to Roman sensibilities that the liturgy remained as straightforward and lucid as it did. Ceremonies of the imperial court found their echo in the church. Especially was this true in Rome following the political collapse of the empire. What was characteristic of the

Roman See became true of other bishoprics also. When they presided at mass, bishops were accorded regal honors which competed with those paid to God himself

By the late Middle Ages the relatively terse Roman liturgy had been overlaid with elements from liturgical traditions north of the Alps, and a new eucharistic piety had emerged. No longer was the bread of the Lord's Supper primarily for the faithful to eat. It was rather an object of adoration and veneration. Communion became more and more infrequent for the laity; the mass was *the* time for their own devotions. The moment of consecration was the only obvious point of contact between altar and people. At the signal of bells they paused in their own devotions to adore the eucharistic Christ. The consecrated host was paid elaborate cult. Such customs as bending the knee in the presence of the reserved sacrament and displaying a consecrated host for adoration in a monstrance* have their origins in this "new" eucharistic piety.

These changes had little effect on the structure of the liturgy, but they gave it the character of an opulent and mysterious spectacle. People watched in awe as the clergy performed the ritual surrounding the bread and wine. It was sung in Latin, a language the

---

* A monstrance is a piece of cultic apparatus designed to display the consecrated host. It is usually in the shape of a sunburst with a crystal receptacle for the host at its center. Monstrances are used to carry the host in processions and also at the service called Benediction.

common man did not understand. Even the lessons were read in Latin, often toward the altar rather than the assembly. Thus even the office of the word could not fulfill its intended purpose.

The architecture reinforced the mysterious aura. Mass was sung amid the flicker of candles and clouds of incense at altars far removed from the people. All were dwarfed by the soaring Gothic arches and isolated by the long aisles and nave. The Gothic church of the Middle Ages was not conceived as a meeting place for a congregation of participants; it was an awe-inspiring ecclesiastical theater where the congregation was forced into the role of spectator. It was a glorious era artistically; the Gothic church stands as one of western man's most sublime creations. But judged by the norms of corporate action, it was a disaster—one from which there has not yet been full recovery. The architecture of the Middle Ages and its heirs has shaped the worship of the Western Church more than we usually admit.

Recalled to Action

With the Reformation of the sixteenth century there came a strong protest against clericalized worship. The Reformers all saw the need for popular participation. Luther took a first step by restoring hymn-singing to the people. He took another by casting the service in the vernacular. Calvin and others of the Reformed tradition gave the congregation metrical psalms to sing and also put the service in the vernacular.

Because of the conservatism of the Lutheran reforms, however, liturgical practice tended to remain closer to inherited models than was true in the Reformed churches. In Reformed lands architectural arrangements were usually changed, and the departure from traditional forms showed a freer attitude. On the other hand, the Lutheran insistence upon retention of the mass form, with the congregation singing the hymnic texts, preserved a degree of verbal participation in the liturgical structure itself not commonly found in the Reformed traditions.

Though practical advance may not have been so great as one might have thought, the solid achievement of the Reformers was their vision of how things should be and their clear enunciation of important theological insights which undergird worship. In this respect today's church is just beginning to catch up to a man such as Luther

Luther saw that weekly eucharistic worship should constitute the fundamental rhythm of congregational life. By that he meant a Eucharist where the people were communicants, not just one which they witnessed. His conservatism kept him from pulling the altar away from the wall so that the pastor could face the people across it. But he knew that such an arrangement is more appropriate. His strongest emphasis, as is well known, was on the regular proclamation of the word. Lessons and sermon in the people's language needed again to become a major focus in the Eucharist.

Clericalized worship was a prime target theologically. Luther insisted that the kind of priesthood the medieval clergy had become was not in harmony with the gospel. If the concept *priesthood* was to be valid in the church it must be applied to the whole people, not just the clergy. That is the way of the *New* Testament. The people of God is a priestly people. All Christian people constitute a priestly order. Christianity, in contrast to most classical religious systems, does not *have* a priesthood; it *is* a priesthood.

This emphasis is usually labeled "the universal priesthood" or "the priesthood of all believers." Note the second syllable, priest-*hood*. If the concept is interpreted "every man is his own priest," its thrust is misdirected. Primarily the concept is corporate, designed to stress the servant stance of the congregation. If applied derivatively to individual Christians, it should be interpreted, "I am a priest for others and they for me." It is an idea fully in harmony with a much quoted statement of Luther that we are to be little Christs to our neighbors. In corporate worship servanthood finds expression in the ancient priestly functions of sacrifice and intercession. Both will be discussed in Chapter Five.

The extension of the priesthood to the entire congregation makes impossible the spectator orientation to worship. It is the effective theological antidote for *spectatoritis.* So long as one can say, "I'm only a layman," it is possible to rationalize for oneself the spectator role. But the baptized Christian must say, "I am a member of the priesthood." From that stance it is

imperative that one participate. The new priesthood
concept restores Christian worship to what it must be:
an amateur activity, an activity joined for the love of
doing it.

As a corollary, any concept of an ordained clergy
within the church must take care not to give it a superior status. There is only one status in the church:
priest (servant). A concept of ordination, then, must
find another basis than the setting apart of a special
class within the people of God. This point comes up
again in Chapter Two.

Liturgy—Life

It may well be a shock to many who think of themselves as "ordinary laymen" to be told they are priests.
Because of the emergence of a special mediating priesthood within the church and because of the widespread
equating of *priest* with *clergyman,* the idea of being a
priest may take some getting used to. But biblically
to call a man a priest is no different from calling him
a servant or even a Christian. Discussions of the priestly nature of Christian people must therefore be kept
down to earth.

The priest image is closely related to the servant
image. They differ only in that the former has liturgical
connotations while the latter does not. Keeping them
linked, however, is helpful to understanding both. Too
many discussions of Christian servanthood ignore the
whole sphere of worship, and too much talk about

worship and priesthood ignores the whole sphere of service "in the world." In the first case Christian service is seen merely as social action, while in the second worship is seen largely in terms of beautiful and venerable forms. Note that the terms service and sacrifice are common to both spheres.

The final task of this chapter is to oppose a view of the congregation or the individual which would divide either one into liturgical and ethical as separated aspects of life. For centuries the church has said that corporate worship is the center of the Christian life, congregational and individual. If that is to be more than a pious phrase, worship cannot be an activity separated from all other activities, existing in a kind of sacred vacuum.

A person is involved in the liturgical action as person. One brings to this action one's talents, experiences, joys, sorrows, triumphs, frustrations. One joins one's fellows as male, husband, father, salesman, Rotarian, PTA member, camera buff. Calling a person a priest does not change any of that. One engages in the corporate priestly action of worship as the person one is. One's life—all of it—focuses in the liturgy.

The liturgy becomes a kind of formal or ceremonial expression of the complex of relationships known as the Christian life. In that respect it resembles a family celebration. The relationships among members become obvious; the things important to the group are stressed and recalled; there is joy, refreshment, and strength from being together once again; there is acceptance of the individuals of the group with their varying personalities, talents, and achievements; and there is mutual sharing of joy and sorrow. But this ideal can only be approached by a congregation of participants.

In corporate worship one's personal prayers focus in the congregation's prayers; one's dependence upon God for forgiveness and strength is shared with the others in confession and petition; one's concern for the larger human family focuses in intercession and offering; one's personal meditation on the Scriptures focuses in lessons and sermon; one's personal thankfulness focuses in the congregation's hymns of praise. Involvement means participation as a whole person, with all that implies for the Christian.

To one who doesn't pray, the formal prayers of the assembly (even the most apt ones) will always seem strange. If the Bible is a closed book for a man, the lessons in the service cannot possibly fulfill their intended purpose. If one has little concern for others, intercessory prayer is bound to seem like a waste of time. The action of worship must flow out of and back into one's life. That life must be of a piece as one lives it before God. Otherwise it is foolishness to speak of worship as central. One hour a week spent in the most ideal congregation engaged in the most perfect act of worship cannot carry the entire freight of one's life.

The only significant difference between liturgy and other forms of service is the circumstances surrounding them. The liturgical role is exercised primarily in the assembled congregation. The servant role finds expression primarily in the scattered congregation. But if both are forms of priestly service, there is no discontinuity from one to the other.

Psychologists stress the crucial place of identity in one's life. People must know who they are. Identity is determined by relationships. Who one is can be stated only in relational terms: the wife of this man, the mother of these children, a member of this community. If the image is to remain sharp, the relationships by which it is understood need continued expression. Identity as father is more sharply focused when the children are pre-teens than when they are married.

Similarly it is necessary for the Christian to identify with the congregation if his Christianity is to remain vital and in focus. As expression of this context of relationships the liturgical action repeatedly causes the person to remember that he is a Christian, how he became one, who his brothers in Christ are, what the life of a Christian looks like. His involvement in the liturgy keeps his Christian identity clear, his purpose sharply focused, and his concern for others sensitized. Separated from the gathered community, commitment probably weakens or becomes misdirected, and the opportunity for renewal of zeal is missing. Of course, all this presumes the liturgy capable of being and facilitating such a focus. That problem is prominent in the last four chapters.

Perhaps the common sense answer is better than
the theologizing and psychologizing: No vital Christian
in this era could for long be content to watch someone else praise God. Motivated by a thankful heart
and a commitment of love, he would be compelled to
become involved

2.

... in a coordinated action

A pistol cracks. The young man uncoils from his crouch, launching himself into the water. Arms reach and pull, hands scoop, legs and feet drive. Head turns, mouth opens, lungs suck air, heart pumps. All kept smooth and constant by thousands of subconscious impulses from the brain. Everything subordinated to one conscious thought: win!

"Try again." The youngster half slips off the pool's edge, arms and legs akimbo, belly meeting water with a painful smack. The brain struggles manfully—arms reach and pull but hands are not cupped, legs and feet drive but not in rhythm, head turns but mouth opens late, sucking in more water than air—but only succeeds in keeping the lad afloat.

Swimming is a coordinated action. The body of a fine swimmer is a marvel of coordination. All its parts contribute highly specialized tasks to the total effort, and their smooth functioning requires many hours of practice.

A bell peals. The organist begins to play, a youth lights the candles, the congregation sings, a lector reads the Scriptures, the choir sings, the pastor preaches, ushers receive the offering, a woman brings a loaf of bread she has baked and her husband brings a bottle of wine, several people lead in the prayers, the pastor gives thanks over the bread and wine and gives them to the people. Worship is the coordinated action of several specialized functions. It is the action of that body which St. Paul calls the body of Christ.

A concept of worship as corporate action embraces more than just the involvement of the people. Obviously each person in a congregation cannot be equally involved all the time. There must be some direction, some procedure. The congregation is not just a motley crew, it is a structured fellowship. Nowhere is this so obvious as in the gathering for worship, the liturgical assembly.

If a person's real life does focus in the liturgy, all his uniqueness focuses there. Paul's figure, body of Christ, is so apt because it allows for uniqueness. He speaks of a variety of spiritual gifts—they might be called talents or abilities—and connects them with his body analogy:

> To each is given the manifestation of the Spirit for
> the common good. . . . All these are inspired by

one and the same Spirit, who apportions to each
one individually as he wills. For . . . the body does
not consist of one member but of many. . . . If all
were a single organ, where would the body be?
. . . If one member suffers, all suffer together; if one
member is honored, all rejoice together. Now you
are the body of Christ and individually members
of it. And God has appointed in the church first
apostles, second prophets, third teachers, then
workers of miracles, then healers, helpers, admin-
istrators, speakers in various kinds of tongues.

1 Corinthians 12

Given today's culture and a church with centuries of
development behind it, one might structure the list
differently, but the point is just as valid as ever.

Diversity—Unity

The people in any congregation—the local concretion of the body of Christ—have differing talents,
potential, vocational experiences, familial contexts.
It is not the aim of the liturgy to force everyone into
one mold. Involvement means bringing all this rich
diversity into the action. Coordination implies a diversity of functions geared together into a unified (not
uniform!) motion. The solution for the fledgling swimmer is not training each part of his body to do the
same thing. It would be foolish even to try, since hands
and legs aren't designed to function alike. The solution is to perfect the proper action of each part of
the body and get them functioning in a rhythmic pattern. It is called achieving coordination.

Involvement in the liturgy should be according to talents and responsibility in the congregation. Hands should do what hands can do, legs what legs can do. It is natural for people with musical talent to be especially active in hymns, anthems, and similar parts of the service. People gifted in public speaking might read the lessons. People with greater sensitivity to the needs of the congregation and the world at large might share responsibility for the intercessions. Women who bake might prepare bread for the sacrament; those who sew could prepare linens and banners. Artists can contribute needful artifacts or design banners and paraments. Young men could be of service as ushers or acolytes. Men of spiritual maturity might assist the pastor in distributing the bread and wine. With a little applied imagination the list could be extended at will.

In many instances the special participation of one person does not preempt participation by all but becomes a matter of leadership. People who have unique gifts become leaders of the others. Those with above average vocal ability join together to form a choir so that their voices can be used in praise of the Giver and for the common good. In the more musically demanding parts of the service the choir may act as vocal representative of the entire congregation. In historic rites, for example, choirs have usually been assigned the psalmody. But it would be a denial of the nature of worship itself if the choir were to arrogate to itself all the singing. Its primary liturgical responsibility is to lead the congregation in singing, to help people achieve a more vital song. Similar examples could be given for other areas, all illustrating priestly involvement in the action, involvement as servants.

The Pastor's Role

The number of functions assigned in a service will vary with the degree of festivity and the talent available. There is, however, one indispensable function within the worshiping congregation: someone to preside over the assembly. What he is called is of little moment, though some of the historic titles are misleading. To call him priest suggests a special priesthood within the church. Actually all are members of the priesthood. Celebrant suggests one who celebrates in behalf of others. The rite is celebrated by all together. Liturgist creates similar problems; all are liturgists. Pastor or presiding minister seems to create fewer problems.

Practical necessity dictates the need for a presiding minister. Someone must direct and coordinate the various functions. Simply put: to prevent chaos someone must be in charge. With several people involved in the action there can be problems in following those famous words of the Apostle, "all things should be done decently and in order" (1 Corinthians 14:40). But the solution is not for the pastor to do it all himself. Then the people are again in the position of spectators. The pastor's role is to train people to perform special tasks of which they are capable and to preside over these actions keeping things in order.

Were the presiding minister merely a practical functionary, there would be no liturgical reason for him to be ordained. A rotating schedule could be drawn and the responsibility passed around. Earliest records indicate that the presiding minister was always what we call a clergyman, and except under extraordinary circumstances that principle has been maintained. Why? Is it another instance of clericalism or a cleverly disguised reinstatement of a sacerdotal ministry* which relegates the laity to a second-class status in the assembly?

In the light of history it would be foolish to answer with a flat no. The sketch in Chapter One indicates the sacerdotal concept of the clergy which prevailed in the pre-Reformation era. And it is not unknown today. Even where a two-class church has been repudiated theologically, the clergy has often functioned as if it were not. The domineering *Herr Pastor* type cleric is not significantly different from the sacerdotal minister.

In spite of perversions, however, the principle that the presiding minister be an ordained clergyman is sound and does not necessarily lead to the abuses of clericalized worship. More is involved than practical necessity: there is a symbolic necessity for the presiding minister which requires him to be a pastor.

---

* Sacerdotal simply means priestly. *Sacerdotal minister,* as used here, denotes the mediatorial, priestly caste of classical religious systems as opposed to the New Testament concept of an inclusive priesthood of all believers.

A full discussion of the nature of ordination is beyond the scope of this chapter. But what follows obviously grows out of a specific point of view about ordination and the pastoral ministry.

History and theology both indicate that the assembly for worship is fundamentally a eucharistic assembly. It is the Lord's Supper which gives basic shape to the action, even though verbal proclamation is also a primary focus. The congregation is gathered around the Lord's table to share his Supper. Who is host at this feast? Jesus, of course. But it is the presiding minister who does and says what hosts do and say. In Jesus' name he offers the bread and wine to the people, declaring them to be the body of Christ and the new covenant in his blood. Functioning in Jesus' place, the presiding minister becomes a symbol of the Lord present in the midst of his people.

The same conclusion can be reached by an alternate route. The congregation is called the body of Christ. But though Paul means that quite concretely he nowhere equates the congregation with Christ. Christ is always the head of his body, the church. The direction of the body comes from its Lord who transcends it. The Holy Spirit was poured out on the church for that purpose: to lead and guide. The will of God cannot be domesticated within the church. Rather the church prays for the Holy Spirit to reveal God's will. How does the Spirit work? Through the word. How is the word heard? Through human proclamation. By the dynamic power of the Holy Spirit the congregation assembled around the proclaimed word is the body of Christ in union with Christ, its head.

It goes without saying that every Christian is responsible for the proclamation of the gospel. But not every Christian is called to proclaim it in the assembled congregation. Some sort of distinction is necessary here between the purely evangelistic function of the gospel (shared by all) and its function of building within the fellowship (a specialized task). Beginning with the commissioning of the apostles, certain men have been entrusted with the responsibility for the *public* proclamation of the word and for its preservation in purity. That is one of the "manifestations of the Spirit for the common good," as St. Paul puts it. There is, then, a group within the church who have this specific calling.

Reformation theology stressed a concept of vocation which saw the Christian's life whole. It resisted attempts to divide life into sacred and secular spheres. One witnesses and serves within the normal avenues of life; one does not go seeking for more "spiritual" avenues. Put in terms of cross-bearing: a cross one chooses is no cross at all—it is rather a most insidious form of spiritual pride. A man's calling in life, therefore, sets the context for his witness in word and action except, of course, under extraordinary circumstances. Most people exercise their priesthood primarily outside the gathered community as they go about the business of selling, farming, typing, teaching, plumbing, homemaking, etc. Their vocational activity brings them into contact with people who need their concern. Here are the front lines of the church in the world; here is the scattered community in action, the same community which gathers for worship, a community equipped by the Spirit for its task.

Relatively few have as their calling the enabling ministry within the congregation. They are empowered by the Spirit to be Christ's official spokesmen within the church. Through their ministry the Spirit is at work equipping the people for their ministries. The pastoral ministry does not carry with it a superior status. The line of division is vocational. One exercises his ministry as a physician, another as a bricklayer, another as a pastor. It is only that the pastor's sphere of activity relates primarily to the congregation itself. As a called and ordained servant of the word he represents Christ to the assembled people. Through the presiding minister speaking as obedient servant of the word they can expect to hear the authentic voice of the living gospel. He represents the head (Christ) to the body (the church) as one who himself is part of that body.

But the presence of the pastor in the assembled congregation is not just a symbol of Christ's presence and activity. The pastor is also symbolic of that congregation's ties to the whole church. Each congregation is a local concretion of the people of God. As such it is fully and completely the church. But at the same time each congregation is necessarily related to the other congregations. To recognize a local fellowship of believers as church requires recognizing other local fellowships as church. For this reason the term *church* can apply to a congregation or to all the people of God on earth.

One of the greatest hazards in a congregation's life is the tendency toward introversion, not looking beyond the four walls of its own meeting place. But the fellowship in Christ is broader than any specific instance of it. In its corporate rites the church has developed ways of combatting the nearsighted view. One is baptized not into St. John's Church, Anytown, Anystate, not even into the Lutheran Church. One is baptized into the church of Christ, what the creeds call the one holy catholic and apostolic church. Paralleling that, pastors are ordained into the ministry of the church of Christ. If we speak of a *Lutheran* ministry, we can only mean a ministry exercised within and disciplined by a Lutheran synodical body. And if we speak of the minister of St. John's Church, we can only mean a pastor exercising his ministry within that specific congregation.

A pastor comes to a congregation as a minister of the whole church. He has already been ordained into that ministry before he is installed as the local pastor. Under normal circumstances (a theology of ordination must not be constructed in reference to desert islands!), when a congregation needs a pastor it does not select one from its own membership; it calls a man already ordained to come and exercise his ministry there. In doing so it recognizes the existence of the church beyond its own boundaries. And the pastor exercises his presidential functions from that stance.

The following examples from the Lutheran *Service Book and Hymnal** illustrate what has been said:

> . . Let us call upon God the Father, through our Lord Jesus Christ, that of his goodness and mercy he will receive this child by baptism, and make him a living member of *his holy Church.*
>
> > *The Baptism of Infants* (italics added)

> The Lord bestow upon thee the Holy Ghost for the office and work of a Minister *in the Church of God,* now committed unto thee. . . .
>
> > *Ordination* (italics added)

> *As a Minister of the Church of Christ,* and by his authority, I therefore declare unto you who do truly repent and believe in him, the entire forgiveness of all your sins. . . .
>
> > *Public Confession* (italics added)

The existence of a pastoral ministry within a congregation, then, is symbolic of that congregation's relationship within the larger people of God. The pastor is a representative of the whole church to the local church.

Our denominational splintering tends to obscure this. If there were only one church, the relationships among congregations would be clearer and this function of the pastoral office more obvious. As things are, we must modify both the title *Christian* and *pastor* with some such adjective as Lutheran, Roman Catholic, Presbyterian, Episcopalian, etc. But the basic concept is still valid.

---

* Quoted by permission of Commission on the Liturgy and Hymnal.

When, for example, different synodical groupings succeed in realizing a high degree of fellowship, we call it "pulpit and altar fellowship" or their being "in communion." These descriptive phrases do not simply say that members of one group may enjoy the privileges of the other. They also imply the mutual recognition of ministries. Where two synodical bodies enjoy pulpit and altar fellowship the ordained ministers of one body may function as ministers in the other. In other words, the fact that they are ministers of the church of Christ is recognized and accepted. In this rather feeble way the symbolic nature of the pastoral office shines through even the present jungle of denominational structures.

Theological heirs of Martin Luther have put healthy emphasis on the function of the proclaimed word in the church. They have also insisted that an ordained minister preside at the Lord's Table. They have tended, however, to neglect an adequate emphasis on the office of the ministry. The concepts of apostolic succession and authority found in the earliest Christian tradition have been too easily brushed aside. Lutheran theology needs a fuller concept of the ordained ministry, and a good springboard would be the liturgical assembly of the gathered community. Out of his presidency of that assembly flow all the other aspects of the pastor's vocation.

Those parts of the service where one acts in the stead of Jesus himself are reserved for the pastor. Since the days of the Apostles that has included absolving, blessing, preaching, and officiating at the table. All these relate to the symbolic character of the pastoral office. The pastor does not do them because he has some magic or mysterious power resident within. He does them because that is his calling—a calling provided the church by God for the common good.

It Takes Work

Corporate worship is not—cannot be—spontaneous. It requires planning and work. A congregation must learn the art of worship just as the swimmer must learn to swim. A human body put in water seldom begins to swim automatically, and few congregations just automatically begin to worship.

There is a difference between personal devotion and corporate worship. It is not a difference in kind but in degree. The circumstances of the gathered community require a different type of action than what is natural for one person alone in his room. Part of the difficulty with understanding corporate worship stems from failure to recognize this. The same criteria which are appropriate to personal devotion cannot be applied to congregational worship.

Take prayer, for example. Personal prayer is often spontaneous and emotionally intense, related directly to the needs or feelings of the moment. It is normal for it to be so. St. Paul writes to the Romans about "sighs too deep for words" (Romans 8:26). Liturgical prayer is less emotional, not often spontaneous, and probably not directly expressive of the momentary emotional needs of any one person. It must be that way. If it were not, it could not be the prayer of the whole assembly. Jesus spoke of two or three agreeing on the content of prayer (Matthew 18:19-20), implying planning. A spontaneous prayer can seldom be the prayer of the entire assembly, since if all are to partici- pate as fully as possible, they must either have a copy of the words or be familiar with them through repeat- ed exposure.

In her book *Footnotes and Headlines* Sister Corita puts the difference memorably.

> There are different sizes of man.
> There is a small man which is a single man
> and a large man which is the community—or two
> or of everyone.
> Something changes when the size
> changes—
> The small man can often express spontaneously.
> He reaches out this way—hugs or strikes
> gets into connection
> and starts the build-
> ing process. . . .
> When groups of humans get bigger—
> too big for a hug,
> too many for a sin-
> gle groan,
> the size changes
> and then the ceremony gets more
> complex and needs to be organ-
> ized. . . .
> For a single man to laugh, the equipment is all
> built in—

one man does something which moves certain
    muscles
            in another man in response, and the
            magic happens.
        For a larger man to celebrate,
    more muscles are needed—someone needs to
        order the cake and champagne or the bread
        and wine
            and see that the musicians come. . . . *

First of all, those performing specialized tasks must
learn them. Lectors must be taught to read publicly,
choristers must rehearse, ushers must be taught their
duties, elders must master the skills of distributing the
bread and wine. Then they must all learn how these
tasks fit together, when and where they are done.

What is done by the people together must also be
learned. Hymns and chants need to be mastered, uni-
son speaking needs attention, and instruction is needed on such procedures as when one stands, kneels, or
sits, and how one gets to and from the altar for the
sacrament.

Baptism, confirmation, reception of members, in-
stallation of officers, ordination — special occasions
such as these require special planning and the learning
of additional procedure.

Most important, however, the congregation must
learn the logic of the liturgical action. They must
understand the significance of each part and of the
sequence of parts. They must be taught the significance

---

* Sister Corita, *Footnotes and Headlines, A Play-Pray Book* (New
York: Herder and Herder, 1967), pp. 3-4

of ritual action so that they can participate in a proper spirit. In other words, they must be taught the habits and customs of the family of God. Some will be local, some universal. But worship is never what it might be until its action becomes second nature. Even after it is learned, attention must continually be directed to weak spots.

This is not peculiar to worship, it applies to any coordinated action. The various strokes of swimming must be explained and demonstrated to the fledgling swimmer. Then he must practice until they *become* natural for him. If he has special aptitudes, this will happen quickly, and he will be able to achieve a high degree of perfection. If he has only average potential, he will always be an ordinary swimmer. But in both cases work is required, and one must think the goal worth achieving to be willing to spend the time and effort.

Even Olympic competitors never outgrow their need for practice. In interviews they say such things as "My timing's been off lately—I'm working on that," "My turns are slow—I've got to trim off some time there." Is it so strange, then, that a weak place in a chant needs rehearsal or that people need reminding about how they are to approach the altar?

Some object that all the attention given to mechanics detracts from the spiritual character of worship. No one would suggest that technique is the ultimate. The superb athlete has progressed beyond the mechanics to full participation in his event. But had he not mastered the techniques, he could not participate so well. His mind would be too preoccupied with thoughts of "What do I do next?"

It is possible to make a thing out of mechanics. The world of music contains many fine technicians who for all their skill do not play music. But it is also possible to be naive about technique. Many a congregation has never been able to participate freely in a corporate celebration of the presence of their Lord among them because no one has taught them how. Technique frees one for the joy of full participation. If a man at dinner must always glance furtively about to see what utensil to use for what dish he can scarcely enjoy the meal!

The alternative to all this work would be to make the service so simple that anyone could manage the first time through. The traditional rites of western Christians could stand some simplification. But it would be an error to move toward simplism. No family gears its customs and habits to the casual visitor. To do so would be a denial of the quality of familial relationships. If the concept of the organic character of the congregation is clear and if the liturgy is seen as a coordinated action of the organism, the quest for simplicity will be in terms of clarity, lack of ostentation and the like. Simplicity does not require stripping away all that is beautiful and rich in meaning. That was the error of the Puritans. A rite stripped to the bare bones would be incapable of reflecting the diversity of the Spirit's gifts and the growing maturity of the congregation.

But what of the average congregation made up of average people who do not exhibit a rich variety of gifts? Are they doomed to forego the real benefits of corporate worship? First, it should be observed that there probably are more talented people than is at first apparent, because the talents have never been developed. Second, there may be great spiritual maturity which has never been given opportunity for expression.

The analogy with swimming is again useful. An Olympic meet will draw a larger crowd than one at the neighborhood pool. Olympic competitors perform so well that they are a joy to watch, and their competition generates a high degree of excitement because of what is at stake. But that is the spectator's point of view. Looked at in terms of participation, swimming is of similar physical value to the highly skilled and the average competitor.

A student congregation in a university community encompasses an abundance of diversified talents and skills. When these are imaginatively employed in the liturgy the result might be analogous to the Olympic meet. Most congregations are nearer the neighborhood pool category. It would be absurd for the students not to use the available talent. But it would be equally absurd for the average parish to try to copy the university services. But how is one to answer the questions about the value of each service for the participants?

If the Spirit's gifts are finding expression in both, then surely the value is similar. Each congregation must be the family it is; it must act within the boundaries of its own possibilities; but it must act.

Same Old Stuff

Variety is the spice of life! That hoary statement has attained an authority almost equal to divine revelation. Many a discussion about the hazard of monotony in the repeated use of a liturgical form has been cut off by quoting it, and people generally assume the matter to be settled. The tacit assumption is: the more variety the more vital the liturgical action. Where the concept of worship as involvement in a coordinated action is operative, however, variety is recognized as a hazard also.

The yen for variety betrays the spectator attitude. Variety does make for better entertainment, as the tenacity of certain TV shows indicates. But it seldom results in deeper involvement. Luther understood this, and it made him hesitant to undertake the reform of the liturgy. In the opening paragraphs of his first liturgical revision, the *Formula Missae* (Form of the Mass), 1523, he wrote:

> . . . I have used neither authority nor pressure. Nor did I make any innovations. For I have been hesitant and fearful, partly because of the weak in the faith, who cannot suddenly exchange an old and accustomed order of worship for a new and unusual one, and more so because of the fickle and

fastidious spirits who rush in like unclean swine without faith or reason, and who delight only in novelty and tire of it as quickly when it has worn off.*

Most stable groups evolve procedures for doing things which remain fairly constant and therefore become hallmarks of the group. Families have ways of celebrating birthdays; nations have ways of celebrating significant events. These are their rites and ceremonies. The more mature members understand the value of this constancy, often at the risk of being labeled reactionary by their less mature colleagues. It is interesting to observe how in times of stress people return to the forms of behavior they associate with stability. For them these "rites and ceremonies" spell comfort and strength. To preface his composition for organ called *Litanies* Jehan Alain wrote:

> When the Christian soul in its distress cannot find words to implore God's mercy, it repeats ceaselessly and with a vehement faith the same invocation. Reason has reached its limits, faith alone can go further.**

Obviously a balance must be struck between a rigid refusal to modify anything and an adolescent fadism. In these years of renewal in the life of the church the latter danger is the greater.

---

* "Liturgy and Hymns," ed. Ulrich S. Leupold, *Luther's Works*, American Edition, Vol. 53 (Philadelphia: Fortress Press, 1965), p. 19.

** Copyright 1939 Alphonse Leduc & Co., 175 rue Saint-Honoré, Paris, owners and publishers.

If a man is to participate fully in a corporate action, he must be familiar with it and have developed some skill at it. Some variety is helpful in combatting a deadly predictability, but if the action is largely unpredictable, he is reduced to the role of spectator. He cannot participate because he doesn't know how, or he is not sure what is expected of him or what comes next. A sequence of unpredictable events prevents learning. If at a dance the band begins to play in a rhythm new to the dancers, participators quickly become listeners. If this happens once or twice an evening, it may be a welcome dash of variety. If it persists through the evening, however, the dance could hardly be a success—at least not as a dance.

A yen for variety may also be coupled with the mistaken expectation of spontaneity. In personal prayers a man seldom puts words together in the same way twice. That is natural under the circumstances of personal prayer. But the same man may expect the corporate prayers verbalized by the pastor to be equally free. If they are not, he suspects that they are not sincere. Free prayers seem more like personal prayer and are thus more acceptable.

As has been noted before, however, it is inappropriate to apply to corporate prayer one's concept of personal prayer. What is natural for the one really destroys the other. The problem with the prayers of the church is not primarily with the prayers themselves (though many need attention) but with the failure of people to understand the nature and function of corporate prayer.

Familiar forms and predictable action flexible enough to allow some variety are an aid, not a hindrance, to corporate worship. Though the hazard of lip service must be recognized, it is not enough to offset the group's need to involve itself as participants in a familiar action and to become more deeply involved each time. "Good morning," shaking hands, "I love you," and kissing carry the same hazard as any form of social interaction, becoming mere formalities. But they can also express the deepest of feelings in an incomparable manner. When embracing his beloved, even the poet resorts to "I love you."

Also at the end of this chapter a simple fact remains. The action of worship is the coordinated action of the family of God in a specific place. If becoming a Christian means being related as a brother to all other adopted sons of God, the family will naturally demonstrate in action both its fellowship with the heavenly Father and its fraternal fellowship. Such a demonstration of love could only be the coordinated action of all.

In the preceding chapters the attempt has been made to describe the nature of the action called worship. The remaining chapters are concerned with the meaning or significance of this action for the Christian community.

3.

... of remembrance

Those whose concept of worship assumes the centrality of the Eucharist must deal straight away with Jesus' words in the Upper Room, "Do this in remembrance of me" (1 Corinthians 11:24). Remembrance, the usual englishing of the Greek *anamnesis*, is a key to understanding the significance of the liturgy.

To understand remembrance as simple mental recall —I remember what I had for breakfast—is to fail to plumb the richness of the biblical *anamnesis*. It must be a kind of remembering which evokes the past vividly.

— having a coke in the malt shop, a coed hears a tune on the juke box which automatically evokes her boyfriend. For them it's "our song." It has become so identified with him in her mind that even a chance hearing makes him so real to her that she half expects to turn around and find him standing there. Even in the future after years of marriage (probably to someone else) the song will have a similar effect.

— a woman passes his seat on the bus unnoticed. But when he catches the lingering scent of her perfume he is transported instantly back to his late teens when a girl he dated wore the same perfume. Just a whiff of the scent brings a sense of her presence which is almost physical.

Experiences such as these point the way into the richness of *anamnesis,* but they do not do full justice to it. They are too mental and fleeting, and they are too private and dependent upon individual experience.

A better example would be a civic celebration to commemorate an important event, preferably one creative of the community, and one which occurred prior to the experience of the present participants: an old-fashioned Fourth of July in a small midwestern town.

People are in a holiday mood; there are speeches which recall the events leading to independence and exhort the listeners to preserve faithfully the heritage of liberty; there is plenty of picnic style food shared among families; there are games and there is music; and when night comes there is a pageant related to the Revolutionary War followed by a gala display of fireworks (a visual alleluia!). The goal of such a festival is to help the community remember the events of the past, give it a sense of identity, affirm the bond with its founding fathers, and provide the occasion for re-dedication to the principles for which it stands. It is a liturgical act of civic *anamnesis* whose ethos is almost religious. Patriotism always has the character of religious conviction and piety.

Were it not for such national holidays and the educational machinery which supports them, important events would remain mere factual data for later generations or be lost altogether, forgotten. The celebration keeps the event alive and impresses it upon the experience of succeeding generations. It keeps the group's identity intact. Sister Corita writes of the consequences when such festivities cease or become ineffective:

> And the people will go hungry and become weak
> and unable to act,
>> unable to express and explain themselves to
>> each other.
>>> They will disintegrate.
>>> They will not be able to remember
>>> together
> who they are (which is what celebration is).
> And so this larger man will begin to do the oppo-
>> site of re-membering
>> he will dis-member. . . .
> And we could move in parallel wise to the great
> man—
>> the whole human running race—
> and see the same thing happening:
>> dis-membering
>> when there is no re-membering.*

---

* Sister Corita, *Footnotes and Headlines, A Play-Pray Book* (New York: Herder and Herder, 1967), pp. 4-5.

But the best example is provided by the celebration of the Passover. After the leader has narrated the exodus story he is directed by the *Haggadah* (service book) to say:

> In each and every generation a man must regard himself as though it were he who came forth from Egypt. . . . Not our fathers only did the Holy One (he be blessed!) deliver, but us also did he deliver with them. . . .

For more than two millennia this cultic meal and the educational machinery supporting it have kept alive among Jews the exodus from Egypt. More than any other single thing it has kept the ancient deliverance from becoming a dry fact in the history books. In its liturgical representation the exodus again becomes real for each succeeding generation.

When Jesus said, "Do this in remembrance of me," he was in all likelihood celebrating the Passover with his disciples.* He selected two elements of the feast,

---

* According to the Synoptic Gospels (Matthew, Mark, Luke), the Last Supper took place on Thursday evening, the beginning of Nisan 15th, thus placing it within the Passover context. But John's gospel follows a different dating, placing the crucifixion on Nisan 14th to coincide with the slaughtering of the Passover lambs. This, of course, puts the Last Supper the day before the Passover. The theology and practice of the church has tended to follow the synoptic pattern, seeing the Eucharist as the New Testament Passover. Since the Johannine arrangement of materials is primarily concerned with their theological significance, this point of disagreement with the synoptics should probably be understood in that light.

one of the loaves and the cup of blessing, and invested them with new significance. The paschal rite of the Christian church is an *anamnesis* of the deliverance Jesus accomplished celebrated by the people of the new covenant established by his blood.

English has been stretched in several ways to produce an adequate equivalent for *anamnesis*. The best solution seems to be *reactualize*. Seeing the Eucharist as a memorial *(anamnesis)* means to regard it as a liturgical reactualization of the saving act of Jesus.

It is for more technical books than this to compare the Hebraic understanding of time basic to this concept with our own. Here it need only be observed that the idea of realizing (even liturgically) an event of past history in the present is difficult for modern people to grasp. What we must do, however, is to see the sacramental celebration as a means whereby what was accomplished by our Lord centuries ago becomes living reality for those who share the Eucharist. The thrust of the concept, then, is not different from what theology has called the doctrine of the Real Presence.

Thing or Action?

For more than a thousand years the church in the Western world has been hung up on the elements of the Eucharist. The reasons are many and complex, having their roots in the philosophical speculations of Western theologians and the typical bent of the Occidental mind. The development was quite natural as

Christianity spread into a world whose thought patterns were different from the Hebraic mentality typical of the Scriptures. But the result was a preoccupation with questions about the bread and wine which prevented seeing the action of the meal whole. The sacrament was regarded as a thing rather than an action. It is worth observing that Eastern Christianity has not been affected markedly by the thing-concept, and that even Western Christianity has not taken a similar tack in its baptismal theology. Baptism has remained an action *involving* water.

Eucharistic debates in our theological tradition have centered on the nature of the presence of Christ in the species of bread and wine. One group of theologians tended toward a "symbolist" view (Augustine, Calvin), while the other has taken a "realist" view (Ambrose, Aquinas, Luther).* Gradually the realist position became dominant, though it took two different forms: consubstantiation and transubstantiation. Those holding to consubstantiation taught that after the consecration the substances of bread and body, wine and blood existed together. Transubstantiation was the view that the substance of bread and the substance

---

* The distinction, though tending to oversimplify, is useful. The symbolist position insisted on a clear distinction between the outward sign (bread and wine) and the inward reality (communion with Christ), while the realist position stressed that the consecrated elements are in reality Christ's body and blood. At least in the sixteenth century these positions seemed to clash head-on.

of wine were changed by the consecration into the substances of the body and blood of Christ.

The thirteenth century saw transubstantiation gain ascendency in the decision of the fourth Lateran Council (1215) and in the denunciation of consubstantiation by St. Thomas. Unfortunately, transubstantiation was often understood in crudely materialistic terms, a view which led to excesses in eucharistic piety. By the sixteenth century transubstantiation had won the field (though not unopposed), and it was the view enunciated by the post-Reformation Council of Trent in 1551.

Luther had problems with the doctrine of transubstantiation as a theological explanation of the presence of Christ made binding upon all Christians. But he was a staunch defender of realism, especially when engaging in polemics against the radical reformers. His defense of the realist position, however, was more along biblical (exegetical) than philosophical lines.

In the Marburg Colloquy (1529), called in the hope of achieving agreement on the Lord's Supper between German and Swiss Reformers, Luther's realist position locked horns with the rather pale form of the symbolist view which Zwingli held. The more faithful transmitter of the symbolist position was John Calvin, and it was his views (which he regarded as mediating between Luther and Zwingli) and those of the lesser known Bullinger which are found in Reformed confessional writings. Until the recent past, then, the realist view was espoused by Roman Catholicism and Lutheranism, while the symbolist view was held by the

Reformed Churches. The two streams which had flowed within one communion had been diverted into separated communions, where they could no longer balance one another.

It would be arrogant to suggest that this centuries-long debate has been wasted effort. Men of the stature of Ambrose, Augustine, Aquinas, Luther, Zwingli, and Calvin were not biblically illiterate fools who merely delighted in playing presence games. But one of the fruits of the renaissance of biblical studies has been to show how this debate has subtly shifted the emphasis of the Lord's Supper as it is reflected in the New Testament texts. There the bread and wine are important, but they are part of an action the goal of which is the remembrance (anamnesis) of the Savior. To ask, "In what sense are bread and wine the body and blood of Christ?" is to ask a question foreign to the mentality of the biblical writers. Perhaps the nearest our current language can come to affirming what they taught is to speak of the bread and wine as symbols pregnant with reality, or to use symbol in such a way that there is no opposition between it and reality.

Sacrament is not a biblical term. But the only biblical way to use it for the Lord's Supper is to speak of celebrating it. Celebration obviously refers to an action, not to the bread and wine alone. To speak of distributing the sacrament, elevating it or receiving it betrays a thingly (static) concept which equates it with the elements. What our fathers were defending in their debates about presence we now know to be the proper concern of the *anamnesis* concept. It is this discovery which has helped the various theological traditions toward a common understanding of what it means to talk of Christ's presence in the Eucharist.

The shift from a dynamic to a static concept of the sacrament had a great effect upon the ceremonies of worship. It paralleled a change in the understanding of the clergy from president to priest. When there is a holy thing there must have been a moment of consecration when it became holy, and that consecration must have been effected by someone with the power required. The thingly concept of the Eucharist is implicated in the clericalization of worship.

The laity in the Middle Ages thought of the bread and wine primarily as objects of adoration rather than food for communion. Though the celebration of masses had multiplied, lay communion was very infrequent. The congregation watched the priest perform the sacred action which produced the holy thing and then paid it worship. In medieval eucharistic devotion the people paid courtly homage to the eucharistic Christ; the consecrated host was regarded as a sacred object to be enshrined and adored. It is fruitless to debate whether the piety triggered the theology or the theology the piety. But it is important to recognize how far the church had departed from the shared eucharistic meal of the first centuries. It had assumed a different function in Christian worship.

Both Luther and Calvin reacted against medieval eucharistic piety. Calvin rejected both it and the realist theology which supported it. Luther also rejected the piety but was constrained by his biblical insights to retain a realist view theologically. The practice of Lutheran churches has generally been free of the excesses of consecrationalism (putting primary emphasis upon the changing of the elements into the body and blood of Christ). For Lutherans it is not enough to "make" the sacrament (consecration), it must also be received. Their insistence that there be no masses without communicants in addition to the clergy assured the return of the idea that the elements are primarily food. But this needed corrective, together with the strong accent on the role of faith, led into the pitfall of receptionism. Lutheran theologians did not ignore the consecration, but their realism was stated primarily in terms of what the communicant received: not mere symbols but the true body and blood of Christ.

In Lutheran practice, therefore, the thingly view prevailed (though in different terms) and militated against seeing the Eucharist as corporate action. Now the problem was not so much the view of consecration which separated the priest from the people and subtly modified the function of the bread and wine; it was rather an individualism which understood the sacrament primarily in terms of personal receiving of Christ's body and blood for the forgiveness of personal sins. The holy thing received resulted in the blessing sought.

Roman Catholicism of a generation ago was plagued by infrequent communions because the laity was content to adore the host at the moment of consecration and receive the benefits of the holy sacrifice (more on this in Chapter Five). The holy thing concept did not naturally suggest a common meal; it was an end in itself. Lutheranism of the same period was also plagued with the problem of infrequency but for different reasons. Seeing the sacrament in terms of individual benefits received (chief among them forgiveness of sins) it was not necessary to commune more often than one needed it personally. There was also the fear that too frequent reception would make the act too common, thus reducing its value as personal experience. And the views of both parties, because of their one-sided equating of the sacrament and the cross, inhibited a spirit of joyous celebration natural at a common meal.

People who have a thingly view of the sacrament find difficulty seeing worship as involvement in a coordinated action. They are motivated to come either to adore or to receive. Where the celebration is seen as a meal in common for the remembrance of the saving work of Jesus, however, the motivation enlarges significantly. The personal value of participation does not diminish but is brought into proper balance with the corporate action. Now the question is not just "What do I receive?" but also "How am I involved?" And the decision whether or not to participate in the meal is based not merely on assessment of personal spiritual needs but even more upon responsibility to the fellowship, upon a consciousness of mutual interaction

Stress on action rather than the elements inevitably

strikes some as selling out the traditional insistence on realism in favor of the symbolist position. While it is true that the present discussion often centers on the nature of symbols, what is held is not equatable with the position of classical Reformed theology. It is rather a legitimate way of transcending the former impasse and returning to a more biblical point of view. The stress on *anamnesis,* after all, cannot minimize the role of the bread and wine.

No attempt is made to circumvent the simple thrust of the words "This is my body" which was so significant for Luther. If the sacrament is a liturgical *meal,* obviously the food is very important. The point is, however, that even the food must be seen as part of an action which involves many other aspects. A meal at which only the host ate, while the guests gazed adoringly at the food, would be no meal at all. Food is normally eaten, not reverenced. Nor would it be satisfactory for each guest to eat with no expression of sharing his company with all present. Meals taken with others normally involve expressions of fellowship. The stress must be upon the entire meal, not the bread and wine alone. Talk about the sacrament must always be about the sacramental celebration. Ultimately there can be no separation of theological and liturgical concerns; they interpenetrate.

Action and Word
The entire action is involved in remembrance *(anamnesis).* But the action is not mute. There are

clarifying words. To communicate to his disciples the significance of the Last Supper it was necessary for Jesus to tell them, "This is my body which is for you . . . this cup is the new covenant in my blood." Without clarifying words an action is to some degree ambiguous.

The function of the speeches in the Independence Day celebration was to clarify what was being done and why. Any observer could deduce from the gathering of people and the nature of their activities that a celebration was in progress. But until someone told him *what* was being celebrated the festivity would remain ambiguous. The action of celebration is rather similar no matter what it signifies. To clarify its significance words are required.

Festive corporate meals are common religious phenomena. There's nothing particularly Christian nor even judeo-Christian about a group of people sharing bread and a cup of wine. As such, a meal which is shared carries a constellation of meanings: expression of intimate social bonds, strengthening of these bonds, occasion for celebration, an expandable circle of participants. These are inherent in the action itself and even carry over into the non-liturgical sphere. When a businessman invites a client to lunch, when decisions are made over coffee, when friends are invited to join in a toast, a sacramental instinct shines through.

What sets the Eucharist apart is the specific significance Christians attach to it. This assigned meaning does not displace the natural meanings but adds to

them, focuses them, gives them a frame of reference.
Jesus himself established the connection—instituted
the sacrament—by his words in the Upper Room
which connected the bread and wine with his sacrifice on the cross.

By theological necessity and psychological pattern,
therefore, what Christians call proclamation is essential to the sacramental action. Discussion of the Eucharist dare not be limited to the meal alone. Proclamation is essential to remembrance; without its con-
ceptual focusing, the meal action could hardly be
understood as reactualization of Jesus' saving work.

In historic rites verbal proclamation takes many
forms: absolution, blessing, lessons, sermons, exhortations, and recitation of the Words of Institution. The
Words of Institution constitute the minimal clarification and are therefore indispensable. It is significant
that all the major Christian rites save the ancient Syr-
ian liturgy of Saints Addai and Mari have included the
Words of Institution, and even that contains a brief
allusion to what happened in the Upper Room.* Under
any but extraordinary circumstances, however, the
sermon should also be seen as indispensable.

At the moment of his conversion the words to the
Philippian jailer were a satisfactory summary of the
gospel (Acts 16:31). But after becoming a Christian the
jailer would need clarification regarding the gospel's

---

* See the discussion in Gregory Dix, *The Shape of the Liturgy*
(Westminster: Dacre Press, 2/1945), pp. 178-181.

significance for his life; he would need to be helped to greater depth of understanding. Similarly in the eucharistic rite it is not sufficient to proclaim what it is (Words of Institution)—its significance also needs clarification. This would be the function of the sermon: naturally to clarify the significance of a specific eucharistic celebration for the life of the congregation and its mission in the world.

The relationship of the sermon to the meal would be misunderstood if it were regarded as a sort of pep talk prior to the real action of the meal itself. The sermon is integral to the entire liturgical action which involves the meal. In fact, the two constitute the major moments within the action. The first half of the traditional rite culminates in the sermon, and the action then moves forward to the meal, which is the culmination of the second half.

The sermon thus shares in the *anamnesis*. Traditionally Lutherans have talked about the presence and activity of Christ in proclamation in a way parallel to his presence in the Lord's Supper. Peter Brunner speaks of the worshiping congregation as caught up in a unified anamnetic motion from the moment the service begins. The entire liturgical action is anamnetic, an action of remembrance, and therein lies the unity of word and sacrament.*

Remembering is reinforced by the secondary struc-

---

* Peter Brunner, *Worship in the Name of Jesus* (St. Louis: Concordia, 1968), p. 284.

ture of the rite and the church year. Such canticles as
the *Gloria in excelsis, Sanctus,* and *Agnus Dei* point to
specific moments in the life of Jesus. The creed
and the formal remembrance of the eucharistic prayer
rehearse the crucial events of salvation history. In this
way the rite presents a wholistic picture of Jesus' ministry as our Savior.

In creative tension with this wholeness is the specific
emphasis of the church year which finds expression in
the *propers* and hymns. On Easter Day, for example,
the victory of the resurrection is appropriately spotlighted, but the rite itself gives expression also to the
incarnation and passion.

The Chasm Bridged

For the salvation won by Jesus to become powerful
in the lives of succeeding generations the events of his
passion and victory must become alive and vital for
them. The events themselves are distant, separated
from us by the chasm of years. Somehow the chasm
must be bridged. It was for that purpose that Jesus
promised and sent the Holy Spirit. Whenever theologians talk of the presence and activity of Christ they
are implicitly talking about the work of the Holy Spirit.
To maintain that this work is limited to verbal proclamation and the supper would be presumptuous. But
these are means through which we are assured that he
is active.

As a congregation engages obediently in the action
of proclaiming the gospel and sharing the Lord's Sup-

per their action, through the dynamic power of the Spirit, becomes the means for the present availability of the crucial events of Jesus' death and resurrection, and thus of God's love. To remember Jesus in the liturgical action of the Eucharist is to become contemporaneous with what God accomplished in him. For that reason preaching and the Lord's Supper as the two constitutive moments of the action are often called *means* of grace. They are that as they are energized by the Holy Spirit's power. The congregation gathered for worship, then, is a general sphere for the presence and action of Christ. He himself gives himself through human words, bread, and wine.

4.

· ... of receiving

From puberty on, American youth, especially males, are pressured to compete, to excel, to become independent, to "make it big!" It isn't surprising, then, to find successful men to be people who are proud of their achievement and their possessions. Nor is it surprising to find among the unsuccessful or moderately successful large numbers of defeated or acutely frustrated people, the casualties of the system. Even though they haven't got it made they do not doubt for a moment that doing so is the ultimate aim.

As achievement has become confined more and more to the materialistic realm, its hollowness as life-goal has become rather apparent. No wonder the mystified Benjamin in *The Graduate* has become a symbol for the younger generation or that flower children with their naive talk of love receive such attention.

The Christian stance is not achieving but receiving. It is the only possible conclusion to the Reformation principle of salvation by grace through faith. Being a Christian is not the result of having made it spiritually but of having been made it by the Holy Spirit. There are no self-made Christians, only self-received Christians. Being on the receiving instead of the achieving end is hard on one's pride.

Baptism marks the beginning of life among the people of God, and like the natural birth to which Jesus alludes (John 3:3) the person is passive. Baptism is received: a man *is* baptized, he *is made* an adopted son in Christ. And while faith perceives and receives what has happened in the action, baptism in no sense depends on faith as if it were God's reward for faith.

In his *Small Catechism* Martin Luther speaks about daily dying to sin and rising to righteousness. It is his way of demonstrating the ongoing dynamic of baptism in the Christian life, a linking of the daily renewal of reconciliation with the decisive event in baptism. The terms come from Romans 6 where St. Paul writes about crucifixion of the "old self" and resurrection to "newness of life." All this points to the open or receptive nature of the Christian life—a spirit not of self-reliance but of reliance upon God.

Being a Christian means no longer living in alienation from God. Jesus' act of reconciliation parallels the act of creation: It restores man to the relationship for which he was created. To be fully human one must be in this restored relationship made possible by

Jesus' death and resurrection. Full humanity, then, is not something native to man, something he's born with; it is received from God. In these terms the good life is a gift, something received from a God who gives solely out of love.

On the surface that sounds great—I don't need to do anything, only put out my hand to accept. After all, it's nice to receive gifts. Aren't Christmas and my birthday my favorite days? And isn't that because I am showered with presents? But in actual fact it is the hardest thing of all because it goes against human nature, against pride.

The embarrassment of receiving gifts is usually smoothed over with the sweet syrup of polite talk. When Dad gives his son a new bike he doesn't say, "It's because I love you"; he says, "It's because you've been such a good boy." The bike becomes reward for achievement, and that causes pride even in a small boy. He may be grateful, but his pride in being good rescues him from embarrassment. Another example is what is said when a man receives a retirement gift from his cronies. Seldom is it given with words of love —unless one reads between the lines—but with such expressions as "You've earned it, old buddy," or "We'll find it hard to manage without you." It can therefore be accepted as an acknowledgment of worth or a reward for faithful service, both reasons for pride. The game is played to stave off mutual embarrassment.

Of course, there are exceptions. Probably they occur most often when gifts are exchanged by lovers, or when a child says as its presentation speech, "I love you, Mommy."

Pride is a strong human passion. Because of it people find more pleasure in giving than receiving. There is satisfaction in having selected just the right gift or booked a table at the right restaurant or remembered to send a greeting in time. Pride makes it difficult to receive a true expression of love which is not a reward and which cannot be reciprocated. And that is the kind of gift received from God. The only possible response is joyous gratitude. A Christian needs all the help he can get to control his pride.

The Christian life, however, is not a solitary experience. Baptism is analogous to being born into a family of a dozen children: it is a personal experience with profound social implications. By becoming an adopted son of God in Christ one automatically is a brother or sister to all the other adopted children. As has already been indicated, this context of relationships finds concrete form in the local congregation.

Because the gospel attracts and baptism incorporates, the congregation itself owes its life to God. In spite of pledge cards, commitment sheets, articles of incorporation, title to building and property, and all the rest, the congregation does not exist as the achievement of the members (or of the pastor). In the ultimate sense it has its origin in water and the word. Corporate worship is a result of God's work in calling and establishing a congregation.

The great hazard latent in the stress on action in the

previous chapter is that worship begins subtly to take on the mood of a transaction: worship becomes something people do for God in return for what he has done for them. When that happens, pride has begun to assert itself. It is as if God's love toward us were motivated by his desire for our praise, a concept which saves our pride. The most crass form of this is a sacrificial liturgy designed for propitiation—a kind of effort to buy off or manipulate God. Propitiation not only perverts worship, it perverts God's revelation in Christ. It implies a calculating or even angry God whom men must please through their worship.*

Because the popular view of the mass in the early sixteenth century came perilously close to such transaction piety the Reformers placed heavy emphasis upon God's action in worship. Luther insisted that the liturgical action was primarily *beneficium* rather than *sacrificium*.** He was appalled by the crass traffic in masses which implied that God needed to be or could be appeased by such repetition of the holy sacrifice.

---

* Propitiation denotes appeasement. To condemn it may seem odd to those who regard it as a biblical term used to describe Jesus' sacrificial death. But a comparison of the RSV with the KJV at Romans 3:25 and 1 John 2:2 will reveal that expiation has replaced propitiation. The accent of expiation is on atonement, making amends for. In Jesus God has provided the atonement for man's sin; we do not, therefore, have to appease him with our acts of worship.

** The Latin terms are retained because of convenience: *beneficium* denotes what is received from God (his gracious action), *sacrificium* what is offered to God.

He therefore repudiated the sacrificial concept of the Eucharist as it was commonly held by his contemporaries and stressed what the congregation received *from* God in the liturgical action. That his corrective led in time to its own difficulties is a topic reserved for the next chapter

Sacramentality

The discussion of *anamnesis* in Chapter Three led to speaking of a Christ present and active in the service of worship. And that, of course, ties in with the present discussion on receiving. What we receive from God is received in or through Christ. Christ is the incarnation of God, or put another way, Christ is the matchless expression among men of God's love and purpose. In Ephesians this is referred to as mystery:

> When you read this you can perceive my insight into the mystery of Christ, which was not made known to the sons of men in other generations as it has now been revealed to his holy apostles and prophets by the Spirit; that is how the Gentiles are fellow heirs, members of the same body, and partakers of the promise in Christ Jesus through the Gospel. . . . To me, though I am the very least of all the saints, this grace was given, to preach to the Gentiles the unsearchable riches of Christ, and to make all men see what is the plan of the mystery hidden for ages in God who created all things; that through the church the manifold wisdom of God might now be made known to the principalities and powers in the heavenly places. This was

according to the eternal purpose which he has realized in Christ Jesus, our Lord, in whom we have
boldness and confidence of access through our
faith in him.

Ephesians 3:4-6, 8-12

A chain of revelation links God to Jesus to the church
to the world. If the world is to discover that God wills
to establish all men in a universal fellowship of love
(that is the mystery revealed), men must find it in
Christ through the church's proclamation.

Jesus himself was the working presence of God's love
in the world. The outpouring of the Holy Spirit and
the concept that the church is Christ's body suggest
that the church is given the same function. The difference between Jesus and the church, of course, is that
the church can do it only as it points to Christ or as it
embodies his Spirit. The church, then, is more properly
a symbol (in the modern sense) than was Jesus, because
while Jesus identified himself with God, the church
can only point to or signify God. Jesus said, "I and
the Father are one" (John 10:30), but the church cannot make such a statement. It can only be an effective
instrument through which God reveals himself.

In some contemporary Roman Catholic thought the
relationship is stated in sacramental terms: Christ is
called the protosacrament (the pattern of sacrament),
and the church is the primordial sacrament (the first
or original sacrament). As the incarnation of God, Jesus
revealed God's purpose to unite all things in him by
making possible a redemption which would be univer-

sal in scope. As a community of people who have been reconciled to God the church continues to indicate God's purpose to the world both by confronting men with the gospel and by being a fellowship which demonstrates what such a people is like.

The figure *body of Christ* suggests that the church is the organ of Christ's presence and activity among men, and it illustrates the unity of worship and evangelism. Worship is the formal action of the gathered community, that moment when the church exhibits most clearly its nature as the reconciled people. Evangelism is the proclamatory thrust of the scattered community seeking to reconcile men to God and thus to bring them into Christ's body as participating members. The church must be *Exhibit A* of the message it proclaims. There must be a constant reformation to conform the life of worship as closely as possible to that goal, and to keep the fellowship as inclusive as love requires.

Sacramentality—a concept quite compatible with *anamnesis*—clarifies how through actions such as proclamation and the Lord's Supper we receive God's gifts. It affirms the principle that God acts mediately, through his creation. To any casual observer corporate worship is purely human action, rather prosaic at that. The sacramental affirmation that a sermon and a simple meal are means of God's gracious action comes of faith. That Christ gives himself to the participants in a meal of bread and wine cannot be proved by logic or discovered by empirical analysis. It is a conviction shared

only by those who share the illumination of the Holy
Spirit.

The Eye of Faith

Symbols — words, paintings, musical progressions,
dance, drama, ritual action — require interpretation.
Confront a novice with an unfamiliar symbol, and he
is either bewildered or he sees only the surface. He
misses the significance, the import of what he sees. If
the symbol is from the sphere of the arts, its meaning
probably cannot be expressed in words, since many
symbols are neither verbal nor have verbal equivalents.
The import (a better word than *meaning*) of a Mozart
symphony, for example, cannot be put into words. To
attempt to explain what a ballet means is futile. Initia-
tion into a symbol system is therefore not indoctrina-
tion in verbal equivalents; it involves penetrating the
surface appearance to the import beyond. Getting the
message requires experience with the medium (i.e.
knowledge) and sensitivity to it.

If this is rephrased, the similarity between art symbols and sacraments becomes apparent: in, with, and
under the form of the symbol we receive its import.
This is not the place to debate whether sacraments
are symbols. Here it is sufficient to note their similarity
and that in neither can the external form be separated
from the import; they are aspects of the same reality.
Both require interpretation or developed insight.

To see in Jesus the revelation of God, the residents
of Palestine had to look beyond the surface appear-

ance. On the surface he was an itinerant teacher making rather startling claims who met a fate typical of in-
surrectionists. It took a special sensitivity to see God at
work in him, a sensitivity sometimes called the eye of
faith.

The passage from Ephesians quoted above says what
had been hidden is being revealed by the Holy Spirit.
Jesus' own promise of the Spirit used the terms of
revelation: "When the Spirit of truth comes, he will
guide you into all truth" (John 16:13). The Spirit's
function is to initiate people into a sacramental way
of perceiving, to enable affirmations of faith.

On the Emmaus road the travelers saw only the surface—a learned fellow traveler—until "their eyes were
opened and they recognized him" (Luke 24:31). To say
that the Holy Spirit leads a man to faith is no different from saying that he opens a man's eyes to discern
God's active presence in what appear to be ordinary
people and actions. Faith further involves the assurance that this revealed God is trustworthy, that he does
what he promises.

The role of faith is to perceive and receive. The be-
liever perceives the presence of Christ in the liturgical
action and can therefore receive the benefits offered
by Christ. Faith trusts that the clarifying words are
true; it says Amen to the preacher's "Thus saith the
Lord!" or the presiding minister's recitation of the
Words of Institution. Luther would have said that faith
sees behind the masks of surface reality to the God
hidden there. These human actions in the service are

God's masks, but only God's people are able to recognize them as such.

Doing and Receiving

The Reformation stress on *beneficium* stands guard against a perversion of the liturgical action. The Christian cult is unique among religions because of its openness and lack of manipulation. There is no holy of holies forbidden to the laity. There are no priestly secrets by which the laity can be dominated. There is no attempt to control God by magic. History, however, shows how easily these perversions subtly find their way into Christian worship. To combat this danger Reformation theology insists that the liturgy is not primarily something we offer God but something through which God offers us his love.

Congregations worship in obedience to God's will. Jews have understood the celebration of the Passover as response to God's command (Exodus 12:14), and Christians have celebrated the Eucharist in response to Jesus' words. The liturgical action grows out of love rather than the desire to appease an angry God. This same action becomes by the Spirit's power the means of Christ's active presence among his people. There is no conflict between the stress on action and that on *beneficium*. In fact, were God's action to be conceived as a shaft of spiritual lightning illuminating a passively waiting assembly, the whole sacramental principle and ultimately Christology itself would be repudiated. That is why Luther fought the Spiritualists so vehemently.

Their type of disincarnate (unmediated) spiritualism struck at the center of the gospel.

Being a receiving people does not preclude being an acting people, but it does insure the proper motive for the action. Being open to God's gifts and dependent upon them is another facet of the relation of liturgy and life outlined in the first chapter (pp. 29ff.). As individuals Christians know their new life is a gift from God. They also know their need for the strength of his presence to live that life consistently by keeping their pride under control. Corporate worship celebrates Christ's presence and is therefore a source of strength. The liturgical action, then, is not only a focus for the individual life, it is also an indication of the tone of that life.

The readiness to receive, both corporate and personal, is in itself the glorification of God. It is no accident that Reformation theology with its stress on grace and faith has as a favorite motto, *Soli Deo gloria* (to God alone the glory). The recognition of dependence upon God is, in Philip Watson's phrase, to "let God be God!"

5.

...of offering

The young pastor opened the door and saw her lying there as if she hadn't moved since his last visit. Arthritis had so crippled her that she could do nothing for herself and so she lay, as she had for five years, looking at the ceiling. But she responded to his greeting with a remarkably cheerful voice. The visits were always difficult for him because he felt so powerless to help. Each time it took an effort of will to open the door.

They talked, he read passages of Scripture he hoped were positive and cheering, they prayed, they talked some more. Not even in her tone of voice was there complaining. She told him how she had been able to cheer up a recent arrival who felt deserted and alone. She told him how hymns and Bible passages she had memorized as a youngster were such a joy to her. She could say them to herself even though she couldn't hold a book or even turn pages. When he got up to leave she told him how his visits strengthened her, how she felt especially close to God when he read to her from the Bible.

He got into the car feeling both uplifted and a little ashamed—ashamed that he had to force himself to go in, ashamed of his daily complaining about petty things, but much more uplifted by the radiant faith of this shriveled little saint. Within himself he asked the question many have asked after similar experiences, "Who ministered to whom?" His visit was an act of service, an act of giving. But in his act of giving he had received much more than he had given. Perhaps that is the mystery of love, that it is difficult to separate giving and receiving.

Chapter Four was a discussion of receiving, and took the position that there is no conflict between an emphasis on action and an emphasis on receiving. Chapter Three described the action of worship as liturgical remembrance. Chapters One and Two investigated the people involved in the action and how their varied contributions are coordinated: the lives of the scattered community focus in the corporate action of the liturgy. In this chapter the nature of that action will be investigated, drawing together several points already taken up.

English-speaking people commonly refer to the liturgical action as "the service." The *Service Book and Hymnal* of the Lutheran bodies use *The Service* as title for the eucharistic rite. People speak of "a service of worship."

But the Christian's vocabulary does not limit the term *service* to worship. People speak about "Christian service" and usually mean visiting shut-ins, making evangelism calls, or giving food and clothing to people in need. Some expand the term to include the Christian's entire life: In every way he can, he should meet the needs of others. That is the point of Jesus' own parable of the Good Samaritan told in answer to the lawyer's question, "And who is my neighbor?" (Luke 10:25-37). The Christian life is not centered in one's self; it is a life of service motivated by love.

In his Letter to the Romans Paul expresses the same idea, but in different words:

> I appeal to you therefore, brethren, by the mercies of God, to present your bodies as a living sacrifice, holy and acceptable to God, which is your spiritual worship. Do not be conformed to this world [or, age] but be transformed by the renewal of your mind, that you may prove what is the will of God, what is good and acceptable and perfect. . . . Having gifts that differ according to the grace given to us, let us use them: if prophecy, in proportion to our faith; if service, in our serving; he who teaches, in his teaching; he who exhorts, in his exhortation; he who contributes, in liberality; he who gives aid, with zeal; he who does acts of mercy, with cheerfulness.
> Romans 12:1-2, 6-8

The Roman Christians are appealed to as priests and told to offer sacrifice. But it is no bloody ritual Paul has in mind; he specifies a living sacrifice. How is that done? By acts of service which correspond to the talents God has given. This leads back to a discussion begun in the first chapter (p. 28): the close relationship between the roles of priest and servant. The Romans passage underlines this by making no distinction in its list of examples between liturgical and non-liturgical acts.

Love binds them together; they are all expressions of love. Love is the motive for service (as with the Good Samaritan), and it is the motive for sacrifice (as with Jesus' death on the cross). When one stops trying to make deals with God, acts of mercy (good works) and of worship (offerings) are freed from the need to appease him. Transaction piety requires the offering of things to God which, it is hoped, will please him. When people receive God's self-revelation in Christ and their actions are thus motivated by a responding love, they can give nothing less than themselves. Love cannot stop short of self-giving, self-sacrifice. Jesus' actual execution on the cross is the external consequence of his total surrender in loving obedience to the Father. Were that not so, to speak of his crucifixion by Roman soldiers as self-sacrifice would be mere fiction. Love is the content of a New Testament concept of sacrifice.

The Christian's surrender to God's will is a demonstration of love. The decisive death and resurrection of baptism sets the pattern for the life to follow (see p. 74). Under the circumstances of the scattered community this love is expressed in varied acts of service to others. In the gathered community one's individual acts of service focus in the corporate action of the liturgy, especially in the offering and intercessions.

The Prayers

By definition a priest is responsible to intercede for others. The love of the Christian priesthood is expressed in prayerful concern for people's needs. Prayer is no substitute for action; prayer is going into action in behalf of others, action which continues in more concrete ways. The individual priest makes intercession for people in his own specific circle of concern. His personal prayers focus in the prayers of the fellowship. Little needs adding to what has already been said about that (see p. 31).

Intercessory prayer was an important component of corporate worship from the beginning. But as emphasis on corporate action declined and people were reduced to spectators, as the mass came more and more into the orbit of transaction piety, the intercessions (as a separate act) declined and then disappeared altogether. Concern for others, which had previously motivated it, was now expressed in special masses. Instead of requesting the church's prayers, one requested a mass for a special intention. After the Reformation had repudiated the sacrificial concepts fundamental to this traffic in masses, intercessions were restored to evangelical services. With the change of spirit heralded by Vatican II, intercessions are once more becoming part

of the Roman Rite (and there seems to be a corre-
sponding lack of emphasis on the special masses).

The Offering

The offering has always been a problem for the
church. It is one point in the liturgy where the entire
assembly is most obviously active. Since gifts are involved, the action seems especially vulnerable to the
perversions of pride mentioned earlier. But given
proper understanding and appropriate ritual expression, the offering demonstrates as nothing else can
the continuity of corporate and individual service.

The gifts offered are symbols of one's self-offering.
Under present cultural conditions money is the obvious symbol for the self, signifying as it does talents
and time (salary), substance (property value), and obli-
gation (stewardship). Offerings of money are not dues
or taxes to support an institution; they are gifts (symbolic of self) offered to God, and can properly be labeled sacrifice. Some historical information is needed
to add background at this point.

In the early life of the New Testament church the
Eucharist seems to have been celebrated within the
framework of a potluck supper called the *agape* or love
feast. Supposedly food was brought to be shared by
all as expression of fellowship, but also as a way of
caring for the poor. From the food for the *agape*
enough bread and wine were taken for the sacrament
proper.

But this practice does not seem to have lasted long.

Disorders of the type mentioned in 1 Corinthians 11 led to the eventual separation of the Eucharist from the love feast, and finally to the latter's disappearance. But the custom of bringing foodstuffs to the eucharistic celebration apparently persevered, though gifts of money also made their entry

The gifts were brought in procession to a table where a deacon collected them, perhaps speaking the name of the giver and saying a prayer over the gift. Persons under the church's discipline were forbidden to participate in the offering, but all communicants were expected to. Since only bread and wine were actually consumed during the service, it was only natural that attention focused more and more upon them. What was left of the gifts was used for the relief of the poor and the support of the clergy.

Gradually the concept of sacrifice shifted completely from the people's offering to the offering of the bread and wine by the clergy (separate from any action of the people). The transformation of the offering into a clerical act, the tradition that the elements required special preparation, the idea that the bread should be unleavened—all this resulted in the virtual disappearance of the people's offering. Vestiges of it remained in occasional money offerings on major feasts (days when the laity would commune) and in certain local customs. Even the extra-liturgical giving of food became unnecessary as the church and its charitable works were supported by income from land holdings, endowments, patronage, etc.

As the mass was sucked more and more into the vortex of transaction piety which conceived of it as a tool to gain divine favor, the people's money was used for mass stipends rather than for offerings within the liturgy. By the sixteenth century both Sunday and feast day offerings had disappeared from most European parishes, and the concept of sacrifice had shifted to the mass offered by a priest for a special intention.

The Reformers saw such masses and the concept of propitiatory sacrifice which undergirded them as striking at the heart of the gospel. In his otherwise conservative liturgical reform Luther simply cut out the offertory and canon of the mass (series of prayers surrounding the Words of Institution) because he found them totally permeated with a priestly offering of Christ to God. Offerings of money were restored in the Reformation churches but given no liturgical significance.

It was to combat this false understanding of the sacrifice of the mass that Luther stressed so strongly the concept of God's action: the Eucharist as *beneficium*, not *sacrificium* (see note, p. 77). This distinction led later theologians to debate whether the Eucharist was sacrament or sacrifice, but on both sides the debate suffered from an inadequate conception of the biblical view of sacrifice.

By the early sixteenth century sacrifice was thought of in terms of the destruction of the victim. Sacrifice meant death. Since the Eucharist was a liturgical act in which Christ was sacramentally present, the sacrifice of the mass was called an unbloody offering. In spite of some sophisticated theological safeguards against seeing each mass as a repetition of the sacrifice of Calvary (now offered by the church), that is exactly how most Christians understood it. Their view fits perfectly with the thingly concept of the sacrament: the consecration changes the elements into holy things—Christ's body and blood—and these can then be offered to God. This is something different from offering to God bread and wine in the offertory. It is offering the eucharistic Christ. Seen in this way, sacrifice is vulnerable to the charge of magical manipulation. Offering Christ to God was regarded as a meritorious act of the highest degree which afforded spiritual advantage to the person for whom the mass was intended.

It was this concept which the Reformers rejected and the traditionalists defended. But it is a concept not congenial with biblical faith, not even that of the Old Testament. Because of biblical studies, Lutherans are being forced to overcome their traditional allergy upon hearing sacrificial language applied to the Eucharist, and Roman Catholics are forced to modify their traditional view and correct a one-sided emphasis on it. Sacrament (emphasizing God's gift) and sacrifice (emphasizing man's gift) cannot be pitted against each other; they are aspects of the same reality. Both the Roman and Lutheran rites need revision to give a proper expression to a proper (biblical) understanding of sacrifice.

Response and Preparation

The offering of gifts symbolic of self-offering is a pivotal section of the liturgy. It has been shown that sacrifice is our response of love to the reception of God's love in Christ. Logically, then, the offering follows the proclamatory section of the service (lessons and sermon). Having been confronted with what God has done for us in Christ (our baptism and subsequent priesthood) and what that means for us today, we dedicate ourselves anew (offer ourselves) to his service (a living sacrifice). We do it by surrendering things of value as symbolic of self-surrender, as first fruits of total availability.

The offering is something people do; it typifies their active participation and, for this reason, is often called the special liturgy of the laity. It can originate nowhere else than among the gathered people. It is not surprising, then, that where the liturgy becomes clericalized the offering receives diminished attention as a vital component of the action, or disappears altogether.

In the offering more than anywhere else in the service, the concept of worship as this-worldly, concrete action is clear and obvious. But two difficulties arise over our money offerings: (1) Gifts of money are seen only as support for the church's work. People with that view often wonder why money should be received during the service at all. Some are even offended by the insinuation of "filthy lucre" into something as spiritual as worship. This objection is clearly met by proper emphasis upon the symbolic function of the money. (2) It is impossible to give clear ceremonial expression to the connection between the money and the bread and wine for the supper.

This second problem brings us back to the pivotal function of the offering: it not only responds to proc-lamation; it prepares for the supper. Technically the purpose of the offering is to provide the bread and wine for the sacramental celebration. Sister Corita wrote about ordering cake and champagne or bread and wine. That preparatory function was obvious in the practice of the Early Church when foodstuffs com-prised the bulk of the offering, but it is difficult to make clear today.

In some places bread and wine are brought to the altar with the offerings of money to suggest their iden-tity. But sacrifice and common meal are related ritual actions. With the sacrifice (the act of loving obedience) there is a shared meal (expressive of the fellowship of love); classically the animal was offered, but a portion was reserved for a meal.* Sacrifice includes or leads to communion.

Sacrifice most clearly expresses the concept of sacra-mentality. What we offer together (bread and wine) is shared among us as heavenly food (Christ's body

*Among the Hebrews peace offerings included common meals (Leviticus 3:1-17, Deuteronomy 12:7, 18), and cereal offerings in-cluded a portion shared by the priests (Leviticus 2:1-16). The burnt offering was a holocaust, i.e. completely burned, signifying praise and thanksgiving (Leviticus 1:1-17).

and the new covenant in his blood) for our sustenance and joy. In the motion from the gift offered to the gift received and shared there is liturgical expression of the mystery of God's action among us: what we surrender to him becomes the means for receiving him. This also applies to the money which is offered and then used to enable action through which God works in the world (social services, missions, etc.).

The liturgical motion from offering to meal is the formal, corporate focusing of God's action in the scattered community. The Christian lives his life sacrificially, ready to be of service to those who need him. This is the practical consequence of his loving obedience to God. As Jesus' own words indicate, one serves God through serving other men. The people among whom one lives and works offer the best occasions to serve God—"as you did it to one of the least of these my brethren, you did it to me" (Matthew 25:40). The liturgical motion from offering to sharing is a paradigm or model of the Christian life.

The Present Task

Evangelical Christians must come to see how congenial their cherished concepts of service and vocation are to the biblical notion of sacrifice. If corporate worship is to be relevant to one's personal life and continuous with it, an adequate offertory section is needed in our rites. The wholistic understanding of life which this would promote would also help bring problems of stewardship into proper perspective. If the symbolic character of the monetary gifts comes through, the idea of dues-paying should be overcome. And if the offerings of money are part of an action which brings the whole of one's life into sacrificial focus, the connection between stewardship of possessions and of life would be clarified. A proper concept of sacrifice could be an antidote to the sacred-secular fracturing of life which makes it possible to wall off Christianity in a separated compartment, and this would help solve all sorts of problems which vex the church.

Transcending the old sacrament-sacrifice division also opens new avenues for the resolution of the impasse of the sixteenth century. Though Roman Catholics still tend to accent sacrifice prominently, they are in the process of rethinking its nature (especially the concept of propitiation). Though Lutherans tend to accent sacrament prominently, they are in the process of recognizing the validity of sacrificial concepts long ignored. Perhaps there will be convergence on the basis of the Scriptures.

It may appear that to recapture an adequate sacrificial concept would be to find the liturgical panacea. Its lack does impede an adequate understanding both of corporate and individual service, and it is crucial to a proper stress on human action as the bearer of divine action. But the great danger it represents cannot be underestimated. Both an understanding of liturgical history and of human nature should warn that being the kind of action it is, sacrifice is most vulnerable to perversion.

Evangelical Christians need to insist, therefore, that sacrifice can be understood only as response and preparation, that its liturgical expression should be centered around the people's offering of gifts. Though there are all sorts of parallels to be affirmed between the sacrifice of Christ on Calvary, which the liturgical action makes accessible, and the gifts we offer, the two are not to be identified either theologically or ritually. The liturgical structure must keep them distinct, yet intimately related. Were it not imported from elsewhere, the idea that the eucharistic Christ is offered by the church would not arise. For the church to offer Christ means that it is (ever so subtly) in control of him, and that, of course, cannot be.

In Christ we offer ourselves and symbolize this in the corporate assembly with our offerings. The offertory provides the food for which we give thanks (in doing so we bless God for all he has done for us) and which is then shared as a remembrance of God's greatest gift, our Savior Jesus Christ. By the Spirit's power, through this obedient action, God gives himself to us in Christ so that the food which is shared is now a symbol of his presence among us. Our act of communion, then, is fellowship with Christ, and in him with each other.*

---

* On the question of sacrifice, see the author's essay, "Luther's Liturgical Surgery: A 20th Century Examination of the Patient," in *Interpreting Luther's Legacy*, ed. Meuser & Schneider. Minneapolis: Augsburg, 1969.

6.

... of anticipation

Hope is essential to life. Studies have shown repeatedly that being deprived of hope is the worst possible fate. Men must have something to live for, something to look forward to. Hope points into the future, and people live from the future. Hope for release has kept many a prisoner from cracking; hope for a break has kept many an aspirant pounding Broadway streets; hope for a better life has kept many in poverty from surrendering to despair.

Hope involves anticipation. People project themselves mentally into the future event. This mental process can be so vivid and satisfying that the actual event when it arrives is pale by comparison. And so people make sage observations about anticipation as being the best part of anything (or at least an important part). Vacations, meals, dates, birthdays, golf games—all these are naturals for anticipation: before it happens the event is lived through as utter perfection. Conversely, anticipation of a dental procedure or an operation may give rise to such dread that one emerges from the real experience saying, "It wasn't so bad after all."

Anticipation is not foreign to Christian experience. Preachers have painted vivid verbal pictures of hellish torment and heavenly bliss, hoping that dread of hell or anticipation of heaven would motivate proper behavior. The anticipation of a life of heavenly bliss helps many a man through a present hell.

Some anticipate heaven with the same fantasy as they might anticipate meeting and marrying the perfect mate. Such heavenly daydreams are truly visions of pie in the sky by and by when you die. But fantasies have only vague resemblance to the true anticipation of the life to come which grows out of the Christian hope. This hope, however, is not marked by daydreams of wishful thinking; it is built on the promises of God.

In the discussion of faith in Chapter Four (pp. 81 f.) it was noted that faith involves the assurance that God is trustworthy and that he will do what he promises. Reformation theology tends to place trust at the head of the list of attributes of the man of faith. Faith is closely linked to hope both as it makes one perceptive to God's promises (the eye of faith) and enables one to trust the promises. The life of faith, then, is not oriented to the past only. Perhaps more so it lives from the future. To clarify this it is necessary to plunge again into baptism.

Under Way

Baptism assures the continuation of the church as the family of God. In the events of Pentecost the out-poured Spirit, proclamation and baptism are seen creating the fellowship. Ever since, baptism has been the demonstrable line between those reconciled to God and those not yet reconciled. In spite of a few exceptions in the Book of Acts, the following generalization can be made: The call of the gospel leads to baptism, and baptism is linked with the gift of the Holy Spirit. Though too much can be made of it, it is legitimate to call the baptismal font the womb of the family of God.

For almost two thousand years the church has been under way from the Resurrection-Ascension-Pentecost to the Parousia (the second coming or return of Jesus). The church lives between the times of Jesus' leaving the earth and his coming again. And this living between the times is the era of faith. As has already been pointed out, faith perceives the presence and activity of Christ among his people—a function unnecessary when he comes again. The testimony of the Scriptures is quite clear that upon his return as victorious Lord of all none will be able to doubt who he is. What is said about him now in statements of faith—he is God incarnate, his death accomplished man's redemption, he was raised victorious from the dead as death's conqueror—will be plain and clear to all.

Those who live by faith now live in a kind of tension: Christ is Lord but he does not yet exercise his lordship fully; Christ defeated death but men still die (even Christians). This tension can be expressed only in the language of paradox: the redemption which Christ accomplished is both past and future event. We were redeemed by an action in Jerusalem centuries ago; we shall be redeemed when he comes in glory. In the meantime we live in a fellowship of redeemed men called the church.

It is not just the church that is under way. The Christian is also under way from his death and resurrection to his death and resurrection. Earlier it was noted how St. Paul speaks of baptism as our being united with the death and resurrection of Jesus, of our old self being crucified and our new self being alive to God in him (see Romans 6). Because this has happened to them in baptism, Christians approach death as people who have already died and already participate in the resurrection life. But that is a statement of faith. One cannot prove that Jesus is victorious over death; no more can one prove that now, because of baptism, one participates in that victory.

Death holds no terror for the Christian because he has already died. Put another way: Death holds no terror for the Christian because he already participates in resurrection life. These paradoxes stretch common language in the effort to express the deep mystery of the Christian life. They will always seem like so much nonsense until one sees with the eye of faith. But citizenship in God's kingdom is not totally future; Christians enjoy it now (though not fully).

To see the paradoxical nature of the life of the church and of the Christian person helps to keep a realistic balance. Being the family of God and participating in the resurrection life are still not the *natural* thing for Christians. This new life remains hidden and alien:

> For you have died, and your life is hid with Christ in God. When Christ who is our life appears, then you also will appear with him in glory.
>
> Colossians 3:3-4

It is significant that ethical imperatives follow this passage: put to death what is earthly in you . . . put on compassion, kindness, etc. The life of faith is a life of becoming—of becoming what we are and shall be in Christ. Knowing by faith that we are God's children, we seek to act like it both individually and corporately. But until this alien life as adopted children becomes natural (in the parousia) we shall not succeed entirely.

Identity Crisis

Doubts come easily into a life lived by faith rather than sight (empirical proof): Is it really true? Is the church really a fellowship of citizens of God's kingdom? Did baptism really change my status before God? Reassurance is needed.

Forgetfulness also plagues the man of faith: my consciousness of the fellowship grows dull; my memory of what happened to me becomes hazy. Remembrance is needed.

Being an act of remembrance, the liturgy keeps alive
the roots of Christian identity. Because of its corporate
nature the liturgical action sharpens the awareness of
identity within the church. Fellowship *(koinonia)*
means participation in Christ and in one another. By
demonstrating its shared conviction and by reactual-
izing its archetypal events, the worshiping congregation
deals with the ongoing identity crisis.

But worship is not just that—seeking security in past
events and reaffirming identity with the present—there
is also a future dimension. The gathered community
anticipates the fullness of the life to come.

Our Future, Our Joy

Taking a cue from the biblical *bride of Christ,* Swiss
theologian Jean-Jacques von Allmen emphasizes the
nuptial perspective of the church. The image is especially apt in its emphasis on living from the future:
the New Testament references speak about eagerly
awaiting the coming of the bridegroom. The church as
bride trusts his promise to come, again revealing its
life of faith.

Modern customs of courtship enable us to take the
figure one step farther. Most couples in Bible times
must have "fallen in love" after marriage, since people
married very young and the choice of partner was the
prerogative of the parents. Lacking our kind of courtship, the bride could only anticipate future love. Today
love is shared during the courtship, but not as fully or

perfectly as it will be in marriage. The church as bride anticipates the coming of the bridegroom as a people who already have fallen in love and experienced his affection.

The joy of anticipation is expressed in corporate worship with language appropriate to lovers:

> It is the language of hymns and canticles, which, for example, bursts forth in the Letter to the Ephesians or which enables the Virgin Mary, when her Son is not yet even born, to sing, rapturously, that God has overthrown the designs of the proud, has cast the mighty from their seats and exalted them of low degree, that He has filled the hungry with good things and sent the rich empty away. . . . This style which carries language to its utmost limits and is typical of canticles, doxologies, and paeans of faith is the true liturgical language, the nuptial style of the Church extolling the Bridegroom and giving herself to Him, and this language is quite different, and must be so, from church language which is addressed to men.*

Nuptial joy also influences the accouterments and surroundings of worship. The garments must be festive (vestments), the best dishes are gotten out (communion ware), there must be music and dancing (chant and ceremony). But beauty in worship is not primarily a matter of such enrichment. The real beauty appropriate for a bride is revealed in chaste and simple word and gesture. Though the church has difficulty in strik-

---

*J.-J. von Allmen, *Worship, Its Theology and Practice* (New York: Oxford University Press, 1965), p. 89.

ing a balance—history shows swings from rococo richness to puritan plainness—the beauty sought is that of loving expression rather than external ornamentation. Joy must find *expression* in external ways (clothes, music, etc.), but the mere addition of such externals does not automatically *produce* it.

When discussing beauty the prophetic protest against externalism must neither be minimized nor misunderstood. Beauty there must be (puritanism is a denial both of joy and sacramentality), but it must be governed by an esthetic which values simplicity and integrity.*

Consistent with the nuptial metaphor, the Scriptures envision the life to come as the marriage feast:

> Then I heard what seemed to be the voice of a great multitude, like the sound of many waters and like the sound of mighty thunderpeals, crying "Hallelujah! For the Lord our God the Almighty reigns. Let us rejoice and exult and give him the glory, for the marriage of the Lamb has come, and his Bride has made herself ready; it was granted to her to be clothed with fine linen, bright and pure"—for the fine linen is the righteous deeds of the saints. And the angel said to me, "Write this: Blessed are those who are invited to the marriage supper of the Lamb."　　　Revelation 19:6-9

---

* Motion picture portrayals notwithstanding, even the worship of the pre-Constantine church took place in an atmosphere of beauty. Gregory Dix cites an inventory of goods confiscated in A.D. 303 during the seizure of a place of worship in what is now Algeria among which were vestments, chalices and silver dishes, bronze lamps and candlesticks. See *The Shape of the Liturgy* (Westminster: Dacre Press, 2/1945), pp. 24-25.

> Then I saw a new heaven and a new earth; for the
> first heaven and the first earth had passed away,
> and the sea was no more. And I saw the holy city,
> new Jerusalem, coming down out of heaven from
> God, prepared as a bride adorned for her husband.
>
> Revelation 21:1-2

If it is true, as many scholars believe, that the Book of
Revelation is structured after a primitive eucharistic
celebration, the figure of the marriage feast assumes
even greater import.

In the Synoptic Gospels' accounts of the events in
the upper room, Jesus spoke of a feast to come:

> And when the hour came, he sat at table, and the
> apostles with him. And he said to them, "I have
> earnestly desired to eat this passover with you
> before I suffer; for I tell you I shall not eat it
> until it is fulfilled in the kingdom of God." And he
> took a cup, and when he had given thanks he said,
> "Take this, and divide it among yourselves; for I
> tell you that from now on I shall not drink of the
> fruit of the vine until the kingdom of God comes."
> And he took bread, and when he had given thanks
> he broke it and gave it to them, saying, "This is
> my body."
>
> Luke 22:14-19*

A chain seems to link Passover, Eucharist, and marriage feast. The Passover kept the exodus a living reality throughout the old covenant. Seen from the vantage
point of the church, it pointed forward to the greater
deliverance accomplished by Jesus in cross and resur-

---

* Compare Mark 14:22-25, and Matthew 26:26-29.

rection. Jesus' victory is won but not yet fully revealed. Until it is, the Eucharist as paschal feast of the new covenant keeps the saving act a living reality among the new people of God. When the victory is revealed (the parousia) the celebration will be like a great marriage feast, and will be the culmination both of Passover and Eucharist.

Eucharistic joy is inseparably connected with the anticipation in the liturgical action: the eschatological thrust of the rite causes the Eucharist to be a celebration. Celebrants are joyful because of what God has done for them in Christ. But to stop there is to truncate the reality involved. By now it should be clear that what God *has done* in Christ cannot be separated from what he *will do* in the parousia or, for that matter, what he *is doing* in and through the church. Lop off any part, and the revelation is truncated. Everything in the previous three chapters focuses here.

To rejoice only because of what God has done results in a one-sided look backward which takes neither present nor future seriously. To rejoice only because of what God will do results in a futurism more like daydreaming than the Christian hope. Rejoicing arises in the life lived now, but lives in hope (from the future)—all this rooted in and growing out of what God did in Jesus to secure that future.

Rephrased in the military jargon which the Bible often uses: We are victors in a world not conscious of our victory, a world still ruled by the demonic powers. As victors we can rejoice because we know that

since its defeat by Christ the demonic is ultimately
powerless. Our joy comes out of the future because it
anticipates the great celebration when Christ's victory
will be public knowledge and the demonic powers
must acknowledge defeat. But, of course, it is Christ's
death and resurrection which have secured the victory
and thus the future.

God's present action is always related paradoxically
to his future action. What he does now shall be done
in the future. He constitutes the church to enjoy now
a foretaste of the reconciled life to come. Scriptures
express this by speaking of Christians in the present so-
ciety as temporary residents whose real (ultimate)
residency is in heaven.

The gathered community is a band of pilgrims still
under way toward their goal, an understanding which
led our fathers to call the bread and wine of the sacrament *viaticum* (travelers' food). Now the term is
usually reserved for the communion of the dying. But
the eucharistic celebration is much more than a spiritual *C ration* for the journey; it is a liturgical anticipation of the life to come, a foretaste of the messianic
banquet. It is a symbolic or ritual action signifying who
these pilgrims really are. No matter how they appear,
they are people who already have died and have been
raised into the new life of fellowship with God and
therefore with one another.

The eschatological reality finds expression in other
ways, but none is so complete as the gathering for
worship. In the formal action of the gathered commu-

nity all the relationships are signified: proclamation indicates dependence upon God's will as basis for action (the "vertical" relationship); intercession and offering indicate relationships within the fellowship and with those outside it (the "horizontal" relationship); the common meal with the pastor as host indicates the interpenetration of "vertical" and "horizontal" relationships. Liturgical action as a symbol of the reconciled community aids it in affirming its own identity and in revealing the mystery of God to those still outside (see pp. 78 ff.).

The jibe is sometimes handed liturgical scholars that they think of heaven as one grand and glorious Eucharist. Be that as it may, it cannot be denied that the life to come is pictured by the biblical writers as a joyous, sumptuous oriental feast. Then there is the prominence given eating in the post-resurrection scenes of St. Luke and St. John. So perhaps a joyous eucharistic celebration is about as close as it is possible to come in anticipating the future life of perfect fellowship.

Our Future, Our Judgment

As it anticipates the life to come, the liturgical action, especially the Lord's Supper proper, stands in judgment against the imperfections of our pilgrim fellowship. It mercilessly spotlights any denial of love. Unfortunately, in many circles this is dulled by the use of separate glasses for the wine. It is possible to counterfeit fellowship between estranged friends or even races so long as listening is all that is required. But when people who haven't spoken for years, have cheated one another, or when people of differing racial groups are asked to drink from the same cup, the crisis can become acute. Here where participation is total it is most difficult to counterfeit fellowship: either there will be a breakthrough to reconciliation, or one will stand judged by failure to participate.

The liturgical action, as has been said, is a paradigm or model of the life in Christ. That must now be amplified: it is a paradigm drawn out of the future. The task of the community is to conform its life to that perfect life which it anticipates.

As a result of a discussion of anticipation, people are often exhorted to recapture the eschatological joy and expectation so clearly evident in the New Testament church. And that is unfair! The hope of most first-century Christians was probably futuristic: they expected Jesus to return during their own lifetimes. No wonder they could be so eager and happy!

Almost two thousand years later their naive view of the parousia is next to impossible, though few Christians would deny the possibility of a momentary return. Christians do not really expect the end tomorrow or next year. When a group predicts it they are ignored as sectarian nuts; when an individual predicts it and begins to act on his prediction he is liable to be committed for psychiatric care.

Lately theology has come to a new awareness of how the New Testament needs to be understood out of the future to which it testifies, and eschatology (the doctrine of the last things) has become a jargon word, even appearing in popular magazines. But the present view of eschatology does not see it in futuristic terms only, nor is it satisfied with the realized eschatology (non-futuristic) so popular a few decades ago. Rather it tends to the paradoxical view which has been followed in this chapter.

The reasons for this new interest are complex. It is partly due to the church's need to come to terms with the biblical material, while finding it impossible to accept it in the simple futuristic sense. It is partly the result of the options which theologians still find open to them. It is also partly due to the cultural-historical milieu with its repudiation of the past and openness to the future. But whatever its causes, the new trend has again spotlighted the anticipatory nature of worship and provided a more mature alternative to the simplistic exhortations. Perhaps the problems with the early Christian timetable are God's way of forcing his people to a deeper understanding of his promises and their resultant hope.

As this is being written the impact of the eschatological orientation is in its early stages. Suffice it to say that the joy of anticipation which led the early Christians to pray with such fervor *Maranatha* (our Lord come) cannot be recaptured in our day, at least not in the same terms. But people shall pray *Maranatha* again (especially at the Eucharist) when they understand Christ's coming to be symbolized in the eucharistic action, present in personal acts of service, and yet paradoxically related to the fuller coming (the parousia). Or it would be better to say, seeing *in* corporate and individual action the anticipation of Christ's fuller coming.

Human acts of love are not mere signals indicating that Christ will come and perfect love will prevail. One must see the acts themselves (liturgical action included) as comings, but comings which anticipate his coming in glory. Now everything is sacramental: his comings are hidden to all but the eye of faith. Then what is now seen with the eye of faith will be revealed to all. What the believing community celebrates in the midst of the larger human community shall then be incontestably real.

> The Spirit and the Bride say, "Come."
> And let him who hears say, "Come." And let him who is thirsty come, let him who desires take the water of life without price. . . .
> He who testifies to these things says, "Surely I am coming soon." Amen. Come, Lord Jesus!
> The grace of the Lord Jesus be with all the saints. Amen.
>
> Revelation 22:17, 20-21

Epilogue

Eucharistic worship is an action with extraordinary richness of meaning. Even an investigation as cursory as this indicates that. In different periods of the church's history different aspects have been emphasized without necessarily abandoning the others completely. It is, of course, possible to hold a view of the sacramental action which is patently false or to perform the action in a totally inappropriate manner. But most changes have been shifts of emphasis.

The particular hazard of the past four centuries has been to seize upon one aspect to the exclusion of others. In the polemical atmosphere generated by the splintered condition of Christianity in the western world it has been difficult for any single group to achieve a balanced view.

But on all sides the polemical spirit has begun to

give way to a renewed understanding of eucharistic fullness. Each of the confessional traditions has begun to realize that it has much to learn from the others. To a greater or lesser degree each has made a beginning at recovering lost or neglected riches.

Recent decades have witnessed the discovery (or rediscovery) of the "horizontal" or "social" dimension of the Eucharist in a way unparalleled for centuries. We seem to be aware of the power of the sacrament, not only to express, but to create new depths of fellowship. Today the right reason for engaging in corporate worship must at least include an awareness of the mutual relationships among the congregation and the focusing there of one's individual life.

This book has viewed worship almost exclusively as the celebration of the Lord's Supper. Obviously there is more to corporate worship than the Eucharist, but it nonetheless remains the center about which the other liturgical actions orbit. The content of the so-called minor services is also found in the Eucharist. Functionally it is as if part of the Eucharist had spun off and developed its own identity while continuing to orbit around the center. Matins and Vespers, for example, are concentrations of the elements of praise, prayer, and Bible reading. Even the so-called occasional services either relate formally to the Eucharist or are connected to it more obliquely. Baptism, for example, marks the actual incorporation into the eucharistic assembly. But even such a rite as the Order for Marriage has its connection, since it affects the nature of the assembly which gathers to celebrate the Eucharist.

Where corporate worship is experienced as a dynamic working of the Holy Spirit among God's people; where the enacted rite is understood as the vital response of the Christian fellowship to the love God has revealed in and through Jesus Christ—there worship will be the rite thing for the right reason.

Suggested Reading

(in addition to works quoted)

Wilhelm Hahn, *Worship and Congregation*. Richmond: John Knox Press, 1963.

Thomas H. Keir, *The Word in Worship*. London: Oxford University Press, 1962.

Nicholas Lash, *His Presence in the World*. Dayton: Pflaum Press, 1968.

Richard Paquier, *Dynamics of Worship*. Philadelphia: Fortress Press, 1967.

Josef Pieper, *In Tune with the World, A Theory of Festivity*. New York: Harcourt, Brace and World, 1965.

John A. T. Robinson, *Liturgy Coming to Life*. Philadelphia: Westminster Press, 1960.

Alfred Shands, *The Liturgical Movement and the Local Church*. New York: Morehouse-Barlow, 1965.

William W. Simpson, *Jewish Prayer and Worship, An Introduction for Christians*. New York: Seabury Press, 1967.

Vilmos Vajta, *Luther on Worship*. Philadelphia: Fortress Press, 1958.

James F. White, *The Worldliness of Worship*. New York: Oxford University Press, 1967.

Constitution on the Sacred Liturgy, Vatican II.

The Author

Dr. Eugene Brand is associate professor of liturgics, church music, and systematic theology at Lutheran Theological Seminary, Columbus, Ohio. Since 1968 he has been a Lutheran World Federation observer at the sessions of the Consilium on the Sacred Liturgy meetings at the Vatican.

A graduate of Capital University, Dr. Brand earned his doctorate of theology in 1959 from the University of Heidelberg in Germany. On sabbatical leave at the University of Cambridge, England, he did research in eucharistic theology.

Dr. Brand is the author of numerous articles on the liturgy and church music.

Tear out and mail

_____
Date

The Book Editor
Augsburg Publishing House
426 South Fifth St.
Minneapolis, Minnesota 55415

Dear Sir:

I have read *The Rite Thing* and found it:

_____ Dull   _____ Helpful

_____ Interesting   _____ Disturbing

_____ Too easy   _____ You name it

_____ Too difficult

I wish that it would have discussed this topic:

I found this part particularly interesting:

I thought it was wrong on this idea:

My occupation is:

Sincerely,

_____
Name

_____
Address

_____
You may choose to be anonymous.